LEARNING
to TALK
TALKING
to LEARN

Linda Clark & *Catherine Ireland*
illustrations by Kerry Millard

Peoplemaking
375 Camberwell Road
Camberwell VIC 3124
Tel (03) 9813 2533

 BayBooks
An imprint of HarperCollins*Publishers*

Dedication

We are indebted to all those parents and children we have worked with who have shared their skills with us. Not least we must thank our own children, James, Sarah and Whitney, who have allowed us to put theory into practice. At the same time we would like to thank those in our families who supported us through so many of our own learning experiences.

Thanks to Derek and Greg for their patience and support and to all our friends who read the first manuscript and persuaded us to continue.

Thanks also to Philippa Sandall for sticking with us and to Kate Tully, Leonie Bremer-Kamp and Kerry Millard for bringing the book to life.

A Bay Books Publication

Bay Books, an imprint of
HarperCollins*Publishers*
25 Ryde Road, Pymble, Sydney NSW 2073, Australia
31 View Road, Glenfield, Auckland 10, New Zealand

First published in Australia in 1994 by Bay Books

National Library of Australia
Cataloguing-in-Publication data:
Clark, Linda
Learning to talk, talking to learn
ISBN 1 86378 167 6
1. Language arts (Primary). 2. Children — Language.
I. Ireland, Catherine. II. Title.

372.6

Illustrations by Kerry Millard
Printed in Singapore

9 8 7 6 5 4 3 2 1
97 96 95 94

Foreword

Early speech and language development will stand your child in good stead for the rest of his life. The ideas in this book can help make the first few years of your child's life fun for both you and your child. You will see how important it is to talk to him, play with him, read with him and show him that you love him. Try to be enthusiastic! If you praise his early successes, he will be more likely to want to repeat activities and learn more.

We hope this book will help you to discover the many natural talents you have as parents and carers, which you can use with your child every day. By combining these talents with the ideas provided in *Learning to Talk, Talking to Learn*, you can be confident of giving your child the kind of stimulation he needs to develop his language and learning abilities to full advantage.

CONTENTS

Introduction ◇ *6*

~

CHAPTER 1

TALKING TO LEARN
Why talking is so important ◇ *9*

~

CHAPTER 2

LEARNING TO TALK FROM YOU
*How and when a child learns to talk, and how
you can be his best teacher* ◇ *13*

Babbling: the first year
First words: 10 to 18 months
Language takes off: 18 months to 3 years
Grasping grammar: 3 to 5 years
Finetuning: from 5 years

~

CHAPTER 3

LEARNING TO TALK FROM OTHER SOURCES
*Other influences on a child's language
development* ◇ *46*

Serious fun: the role of play
The rhythm section: the role of music and other sounds
Read any good books lately?: the role of books
Rounded individuals or square eyes?: the role of television

CHAPTER 4

LEARNING TO TALK IN SPECIAL SITUATIONS
Language development in more challenging environments ◇ *78*

Parlez-vous English?: growing up bilingual
The more the merrier: multiple birth children

~

CHAPTER 5

TALKING ABOUT BEHAVIOUR
Using speech to encourage positive behaviour ◇ *87*

~

CHAPTER 6

COMMON QUESTIONS ABOUT TALKING ◇ *99*

~

Appendices ◇ *116*

APPENDIX I
Children's booklist
APPENDIX II
Further reading for parents and carers
APPENDIX III
Bibliography

Index ◇ *126*

INTRODUCTION

~

Most of us take learning to talk for granted, yet all parents know the thrill — and the wonderful sense of achievement — when our children begin to talk to us.

Speech and language development is the basis on which all other skills develop. Language refers to all the different ways we communicate, including not only the way we talk but the way we listen, gesture, read and write.

To understand the world around them, children must have names for people, things and actions. They need to reason why and when things happen and even to manipulate people and events.

Studies of language development have shown beyond doubt that early development of speech is the one skill that will stand children in good stead for the rest of their lives; early sitting, walking or first teeth, on the other hand, do not have any relevance to later academic ability. Whilst late talkers do not always have problems in the classroom, it is very rare for early skilled talkers to have learning difficulties.

As parents, most of us do things as a matter of course to help our children learn to talk. However, without an understanding of how language develops we can sometimes put obstacles in the way or not take advantage of certain situations.

The aim of this book is to give you the information, ideas, activities and skills required to boost your child's language and learning abilities. It is not aimed at creating a 'genius' or turning you into a formal teacher, but at helping you make the most of your child's enormous potential.

Learning to Talk, Talking to Learn is for all parents and carers who want to help young children — especially in their first four years — learn to talk and talk better or earlier than they might otherwise have done. It will show you how to:

- teach your child to talk, in a relaxed and practical way;
- expand your child's speech and language skills by always keeping one step ahead;
- expand your child's vocabulary and general knowledge;
- encourage your child to want to learn;
- expand your child's learning potential;
- make communication easier;
- make communication more fun for your child and your family;
- enjoy your child more as he develops.

As speech pathologists we have worked for a number of years with children who have problems with speech and language development, including those:

- who are late in speaking;
- whose speech is unclear;
- who are non-fluent or who stutter;
- who have difficulty understanding what is said to them;
- who have problems with their grammar and vocabulary.

Drawing on our experience as speech pathologists and as parents, we are going to show you how you can use everyday situations and relaxed, happy play time to help your child learn to talk. In doing this you can help prevent speech and language problems, increase learning potential and enjoy your child. It is not difficult or time-consuming: virtually all parents and carers have the ability and the time to talk to their children.

LINDA CLARK, CATHERINE IRELAND

Please note that throughout this book the word 'he' has been used to mean both 'he' and 'she'. The book has been written this way for ease of reading and understanding.

CHAPTER ONE

TALKING TO LEARN

Why talking is so important

Communication skills are arguably the most important skills we can gain in life. The nature of our communication skills will affect our relationships, education, employment opportunities — every aspect of our lives.

Our views of people are often based on our first impressions of the way they look and speak. We have found that teachers often use a child's verbal skills as a measure of his abilities. Whether we like it or not, a child may be labelled 'slow' or 'bright' because of the way he talks.

Think about how you communicate. You need to listen, take turns, understand what is said to you, create your own ideas, and have the vocabulary and grammar to express yourself. Even the sequence of your sounds, words and ideas is important. Your child, too, needs to learn all this just to talk.

Following are some of the vital things children are learning to do as they develop into special little individuals. You'll see how talking plays an integral part in each of them.

Asking for things he wants

We see many young children who are unable to ask for a drink or a toy. They resort to pointing, pulling and screaming to try to tell their parents what they want. The poor parent can only try to guess. Both parents and child end up feeling exhausted and frustrated. How much easier it would be if he could say 'drink please'.

Seeking information and so learning about new things

As parents we have all been worn down by the two-year-old with the constant 'what's that?' or the three- or four-year-old asking 'why?' But this is their way of finding out what things are and how things happen. Likewise, playing with a toy that requires a child to do something in order for it to work encourages him to have a more enquiring mind.

Talking about experiences, feelings and things about himself

By talking about their likes, fears and moods, children learn to deal with their feelings and emotions. Once the child has verbalised such feelings we can provide appropriate support and aim to increase his emotional security.

Young children love to give their opinions on all sorts of subjects. One of our children has always been very quick to offer an opinion on her mother's clothes: 'Mum, that colour just doesn't look good on you. I like the blue jumper better.' Dare we say, she is often right! This form of language reflects your child's personality, showing preferences and an interest or lack of it.

Talking to themselves about what they are doing or what they are going to do can also encourage children to express feelings and emotions more openly. Thinking aloud is another way young children begin to express more about themselves.

Developing social skills including making friends and enlisting the help of others

The way we use our talking can influence the way others respond to us. If my spouse said 'get me a newspaper' my response would be 'go and get it yourself'. This doesn't help the relationship. A more tactful and polite approach may have got him the newspaper.

A child can learn how to use his talking more effectively. Learning how to greet friends is important: a 'Hey! You!' shouted across the kindergarten playground may not entice peers to join in with your child's play.

Having a friend join in is not the only objective; a child must also learn to use his language to gain his turn, offer to share, take turns in conversation and play cooperatively.

Young children can also learn to make jokes and tease appropriately as well as how to sympathise: 'Oh no. Is your finger hurting? I'll go and ask the teacher for a bandaid.'

Enjoying using language to create an imaginary world

The 'let's make believe' world of children provides a safe environment for them to try out different ways of communicating. Playing mummies and daddies or schools enables the child to experience different roles, such as being boss or being naughty.

Whilst an active imagination is sometimes frowned upon, life would be very boring without the new ideas and inventions that such imaginations produce.

Making his own decisions and thinking independently

Teaching our children to make decisions and solve problems helps develop their ability to think independently. As parents we can provide problem-solving practice in everyday

The 'let's make believe' world of children provides a safe environment for them to try out different ways of communicating.

routines. We can discuss alternative solutions and resolve the problem out loud: 'What would you like for dessert? Peter is having fruit but you can have fruit or ice cream.'

Life is full of situations where the rules are inappropriate. As parents we often ask our children to do things, expecting them not to take us literally but to apply their own judgement to the situation.

We were once at a friend's place when the mother and her daughter were making toast for lunch. The telephone rang and the mother called to her daughter to watch the toast. She did just as she was told and watched the toast burn and catch alight. Unfortunately the daughter did not make an independent decision.

There may be times where taking the initiative may be crucial to a child's safety. If told 'never speak to strangers', a child may be afraid to seek help in dangerous situations.

Taking important steps towards reading

If a child's talking is limited and unclear it may be much harder for them to make sense of the written word. If we think of the written word as an extension of talking, then reading will clearly be easier for a child with good verbal skills.

~

CHAPTER TWO

LEARNING TO TALK FROM YOU

How and when a child learns to talk, and how you can be his best teacher

Learning to talk doesn't begin with the child's first words but long before that — from the time of birth and possibly even before. Babies have a built-in interest in listening to voices and will start to grasp language long before they can use it themselves. This is the first thing to appreciate in helping a child learn to talk: understanding is always one step ahead of talking. Becoming familiar with more complex words and sentences is how we all learnt to eventually use them ourselves.

Think about people learning a foreign language. It is generally accepted that their understanding is about six months ahead of their speech. If you apply that rule-of-thumb to children, and take account of the vast amount they learn in six months at this steep part of life's learning curve, you will begin to see just how much we may not give them credit for!

Learning to talk, then, is largely dependent on being stimulated with words and sentences of ever-increasing complexity. The bulk of this stimulation comes from a child's parents and other regular carers.

So how do we stimulate? Do we just talk all the time? Talking to babies who can't answer back is easier for some people than for others who feel very self-conscious. And anyway, is this really all we have to do?

Fortunately, parents are natural teachers and, equipped with a basic understanding of how children learn to talk, you can provide just the right type of stimulation at each stage of your child's development.

Certainly, this stimulation is not just a matter of 'any talking will do'. Dr Paula Menyuk, Director of the Language Behavior Program at Boston University's School of Education, studied communication in 56 families with young children. She reported that language skills were better developed in the children whose parents spoke to them directly and allowed them time to respond than in those whose parents simply talked all the time. Menyuk showed that it is possible for parents to overstimulate so that there is no noticeable benefit to their child's language development. The child appears to 'switch off' to constant chatter, which becomes background noise rather like television can be. More structured conversation, on the other hand, was shown to benefit the child's language growth substantially.

'Structured conversation' might sound formal, but it doesn't mean you have to sit down and have a speech lesson. Everyday activities provide the best experiences for language development. Get into the habit of telling your child all the things you are doing, what you are using and what comes next. Talk whilst you are sweeping the floor. Show your toddler the 'broom', let him try pushing it 'up' and 'down'.

Everyday activities provide all the opportunities you need for dialogue, questions and answers, and carrying out commands, as well as giving you appropriate settings in which to name objects:

'Look, John. Look, a potato. It's a big potato. Hold the potato. Shall I cut it? I'll cut up the potato and put it into the saucepan. Look at the potato.'

This helps your child learn that talking is about things, and that things have names which are useful.

Try to avoid constant background and other noise when you're encouraging your child to talk. It is hard for him to pay attention to you with television and other noises in the same room. This is particularly important for second and subsequent children as they have fewer opportunities for uninterrupted one-to-one conversation. This is one of the reasons subsequent children tend to speak later than first-borns. If you are aware of this, you can minimise the effect.

Listen carefully to your child and try to answer every time he 'talks' to you. You don't need to stop what you're doing every time he makes a noise, but speech will increase if your child believes that talking gets results.

Make every effort to understand him when you see that he's trying to communicate. If he doesn't have the words to explain, ask if he can show you what he means.

Communication skills

Communication is the sharing of information, desires and ideas. It is a two-way interaction: both the speaker and the listener need to be able to send, receive and understand messages in order to communicate effectively. Talking is only one way of communicating a message - other means include gesturing, reading and writing.

In order to communicate by talking, a child needs to learn competence in a number of areas:

Articulation: the use of the tongue, lips,

How language develops

0 TO 3 MONTHS	Cries, makes eye contact, smiles. Responds to sounds.
3 TO 6 MONTHS	Makes a variety of noises that sound more like speech. Also uses a range of non-speech sounds such as squealing and yelling. Recognises the difference between angry and friendly voices.
6 TO 12 MONTHS	Recognises common objects by name. Uses simple gestures like clapping hands, shouts to attract attention. Babbling becomes more complex. Begins to use facial expression (such as eye gazes), vocalisation and gestures (reaching, pointing) to communicate.
12 TO 18 MONTHS	Starts to use lots of single words, although they may not be clearly spoken.
18 MONTHS TO 2 YEARS	Understands a lot of what is said to him, starts using little sentences.
2 TO 3 YEARS	Quantity of speech greatly increases. Talks about events in the 'here and now'. Becoming quite skilled at conversation. Takes turns speaking and listening. Responds to directions and questions. By three years, strangers should *understand* your child most of the time, although errors are still made with sounds.
3 TO 5 YEARS	Makes sentences and tells stories. Has a very large vocabulary and can use sentences of eight or more words. Can relay information. Can talk about events that happened yesterday or will happen tomorrow. Constantly asks questions.
5 TO 7 YEARS	Your child talks almost as well as you. All sounds are produced clearly. Occasional errors are made with irregular verbs ('broked' instead of 'broken'). Vocabulary continues to expand.

teeth and palate to form speech sounds. Articulation develops over the period between five and seven years.

Language: the system of rules which govern the words we use. English has hundreds of rules which our children need to learn. For example, we add an 's' for plurals and use 'is' with 'ing' endings when talking about the present, as in 'he is sitting'. There are also many exceptions to the rules!

Comprehension: the understanding of language. Verbal comprehension is when a child can relate a spoken word to a meaningful object in any form or context: he knows when someone says 'cup' that they are referring to the object from which he drinks. A child needs to understand language before he can use speech effectively.

Expression: the way we convey an idea using a combination of words, intonation and body language. The intonation and body language help give meaning to the words spoken: I may talk about a *black*bird or a black *bird*, and I certainly wouldn't expect much response from my child if I told him off using a gentle tone of voice and with a smile on my face.

Sequencing: being able to put sounds, words and eventually ideas into the correct order for the listener to understand. For example with sounds, the four-legged furry animal which meows is a c-a-t not an a-c-t or a t-a-c. Regarding words, imagine the listener's reaction if you said 'Table the on hat is the'. Similarly with ideas, it would be confusing to tell the story: 'He was tossed off when he hit a stone. The boy was riding his bike. His leg is in plaster. He was rushed to hospital.' Our sounds, words and ideas need to be sequenced to convey information. Like writing a story, we use a beginning, a middle and an end.

Listening: paying attention to the sounds you hear so that you can interpret their meaning. This is different from hearing, which is an automatic physical response to a stimulus. We all know children — and indeed some adults! — who have nothing physically wrong with their hearing but who don't seem to listen.

Intonation: the 'music' in your voice, the way it goes up and down and stresses certain syllables. Intonation can change the meaning of a word. For example, by changing intonation we can say 'yes' to mean 'definitely yes', 'maybe', 'if I have to' or 'who is it?'.

Babbling

The first year

A newborn baby's only form of communication is crying. In the first days it may seem to you that all his cries are the same, but in fact he has a repertoire of different cries to express his needs and feelings, which you will very quickly learn to distinguish. For example, you will immediately recognise a sudden cry of pain — it will make you stop whatever you're doing and rush immediately to the baby.

A baby can hear from the moment of birth. Loud, sudden sounds will make his body jump, while he will often show his pleasure at a regular rhythmical voice. From the first days of life, a baby responds to the nature of sounds, and most particularly to the tone of your voice. He will be soothed by soft, caressing tones and upset by a loud, harsh voice. Watch how attentive your baby is to your voice. He might hear all sounds but he *listens* with obvious concentration to voices. If he is lying still when you begin to speak, he will start to move excitedly.

Just as voices are the most important things for babies to listen to, so faces are the most important things for them to look at. Remember that babies can only focus on objects that are about half an arm's length away.

Speak directly to your baby from this distance and see how he watches the movement of your lips. With his careful attention to your tone of voice and your movements, your baby is already learning about talking.

At around six weeks, a baby begins to respond to being smiled at and talked to: he will smile and kick and generally show signs of pleasure. By around two months he adds some sounds of his own, and by three months he has sorted out smiling from talking, so that he smiles back at smiles and talks back at speech.

When your baby reaches this lovely stage you can spend many happy periods cooing and gurgling together, taking turns listening and making sounds. This enjoyable game is important for language learning as it practises the turn-taking

With his careful attention to your tone of voice and your movements, your baby is already learning about talking.

of conversation which your baby will need later on. Babies do not respond to other noises in this way, only to familiar voices.

Babies who are talked to a great deal are much more likely to be talkative children, while those who are handled in silence talk much less, which has implications for their social interactions and other learning experiences.

Of course, babies don't only speak when spoken to, they will chatter away to themselves for hours in their cots and prams. Although you can't understand a word of it, you will notice how your baby maintains the conversational rhythm: he makes a sound, pauses as if to listen and then 'responds'.

By about six months he will start linking streams of his sounds together to 'babble'. With practice, his babbling becomes more and more complicated — talk to your baby to help him extend his range of sounds.

By around eight months most babies have started to take greater interest in

adult conversation, even when it is not directed at them. When sitting between two adults, your baby might turn his head as if at a tennis match as each person speaks. But he won't be left out for long. Soon he will contribute his own chatter to the conversation or let out a shout to regain attention. At this stage, his speech is beginning to mimic the inflection of adult conversation; you will notice that it often sounds like he's asking a question. Include him in your conversations, listen to his babbling and when he pauses in anticipation, respond with an 'answer'.

While babbling does not influence the age at which first words are used, it does help babies practise sound combinations, so babbling to your baby is actually serving a very important purpose, as well as being fun.

Don't panic if your child doesn't babble. Whilst most children do, there are others who don't say anything until they can utter a (reasonably) recognisable word.

Watch your baby closely: pointing, eye gazing and crying all have meaning too and you can encourage him to communicate more by showing that you understand what he wants or feels and by showing that there are words to describe these things.

Remember that the understanding of speech develops prior to talking. Your child cannot learn to ask for an object until he knows what it is called. From as early as six to nine months you can start

repeating common words in a way that will teach your baby the association between the sound and the object or action. Use short sentences and pause frequently:

'Look at the onion.
Mmmm, smell the onion.
I'll take the skin off.
Now I'll chop the onion.'

This technique is discussed at some length in the following section.

It is never too early to read to your baby. You know already how much he enjoys listening to the tone and expression in your voice. Reading to a young baby involves close physical contact which provides a positive atmosphere. Even reading aloud from a good novel in the early days will help your baby listen and attend to voices as something special. Read dramatically, over-emphasising the rhythm. When your baby is able, move onto clearly-defined, uncluttered books. Point to and talk about the pictures as if the baby was older. Tell him the names of the things you are looking at.

Begin to encourage his listening skills, too. When you hear an everyday sound such as the telephone, lawnmower or the bath running, ask your child what it is and discover the source of the sound together.

All of this will help guide your baby towards uttering his first words.

First words
10 to 18 months

First words are usually the names of people, animals or objects which are of interest to your child, as well as useful words like 'more' and 'up'.

When you feel your child is getting ready to make his first attempts at meaningful speech, it can be helpful to choose half a dozen words and concentrate on these. Words that can be used often — such as 'Daddy' and 'milk' — will get the best results. The 'First words' table on page 25 will give you plenty of other ideas.

Relevance and repetition are very important at this stage. You need to show your child what the word means and to say it for him repeatedly. For example, when he holds out his cup for more juice, ask 'More? More?', and then pause. Then pour him more juice and explain: 'More!'. Eventually he will imitate your word when you pause for his response.

Similarly, when you go to pick him up from the floor you might ask 'Up?' and then pause. When you pick him up, you exclaim 'Up!' in an exaggerated voice. He will begin to realise that when he wants you to get him off the floor, the relevant word is 'up'.

Simple games such as 'clap hands' are also useful at this stage. Your child will learn that when you say those two words, you are describing the action of putting his hands together.

Once your child shows an interest in learning to talk, try to keep your conversations with him as simple as possible. It is very confusing to the child if every object is named but each name mentioned only once. Similarly, if the words form a long, complex sentence, the meaning can be lost on him entirely. For example, it is much easier to learn the meaning of 'more' in the situation described above than from a question such as 'Would you like some more juice to drink, darling?'.

A child's first real words are often very difficult to identify. Listen carefully to your child's babbling and see whether he uses a sound consistently: is he trying to say a word? Children learning to talk often think that any word will do and insistently use their own words: for instance, 'bop' might mean 'milk'. If it is used consistently, then you should regard it as your child's own special word for that object.

Also, a child at this early stage will often substitute easier sounds for more difficult ones ('doo' for 'shoe') or miss out sounds at the beginning or end of words ('do' for 'dog').

As your child shows more and more interest in words, keep focussing on objects that he finds useful or interesting. Don't worry if a word seems difficult. It will be harder getting him to say 'ball' if all he is interested in is a toy dinosaur.

Who cares how he pronounces it at first!

Once your child starts to talk, it is worth making a list of the words he can say. You will possibly be very surprised how many there are.

You will notice that your child's meaning is not always the same as the adult meaning of a word: 'dog' may be any four-legged animal, or 'ball' may be reserved for his very own ball.

When your child can use some words, you can set up situations where he can practise them. If he's saying 'hat', devise a game using different hats. Keeping in mind that understanding precedes talking, such situations are also a good time to introduce more complexity in the form of qualifying words. When your child says 'hat', say 'yes, big hat' or 'yes, Peter's hat'.

As part of using words appropriately, your child will also learn to use his tone of voice to convey different meanings. It is up to the listener to interpret the meaning! When he says 'Daddy', he might mean:

Come here, Daddy!
Where's Daddy?
There's Daddy.
Great! Here's Daddy!
Don't, Daddy!

DADDY?

Activities to encourage first words

- Listen for everyday sounds and ask your child 'What's that?'. Encourage your child to listen carefully and to guess what is making the sound. Then track it down and discover the source of the sound.

- Stand toys, one at a time, on the lid of a box. When your child is watching, make the toys fall into the box and exclaim 'Gone!'.

- When playing with blocks, make the most of opportunities to use words like 'up', 'more' and 'all fall down'.

- Have a tea party with all the dolls and teddies. Offer each toy a drink or biscuit with the same repetitive question: 'More drink?', 'More biscuit?'.

- Find and name parts of the body, with or without rhymes. Make it more difficult by asking your child to find 'your eyes' and 'my eyes'.

- Use often-repeated phrases with exaggerated intonation: 'Where are you?' when looking for any person or object.

- Don't forget to name actions as well as naming objects: 'Come and eat'.

- Provide words to express feelings and to get help. Draw pictures of teddies looking sad, cross, happy and surprised.

- Show your child how to blow bubbles. It is actually quite difficult for young children, but good practice for later speech production. It also provides an opportunity to teach words like 'more', 'bubbles', 'pop' and 'gone'.

- Hold your baby's hand and wave goodbye from as young as two or three months.

PEOPLE	OBJECTS	LOCATION WORDS	ACTIONS	MODIFIERS	SOCIALLY USEFUL
Mummy	apple	up	kiss	more	bye-bye
Daddy	ball	down	sleep	my	hi
Baby	bikky	there	gimme	your	hello
Family names	bus	here	want	big	no
....	car	in	wash	little	please
....	cup	on	eat	mine	thanks
....	comb	that	drink	hot	ta
	chair	this	sit	wet	
Child's name	dolly		down	that	
Teacher's name	shoe		fall	this	
....	spoon		comb/brush	a	
....	sweets		gone/all gone	yuk!	
	teddy		go		
	bath		stop		
Names of pets	man		throw		
....	bed		up		
....	eye		in		
	key		do		
Favourite toys	door		open		
....	dog		fix		
....	sock		come		
	TV		look		
Pronouns	book				
Me	light				
I	tree				
You	see-saw				
Mine	clock				

From *Learning to Talk*, Macquarie University.

Helping your one-year-old learn to talk

- Talk to him about anything — people, things, activities.
- Show him what you are talking about.
- Use short, simple, clear sentences to label and expand his world.
- Repeat a lot.
- Allow him time to talk.
- Copy his sounds, as if having a conversation.
- Be animated and vary your voice and facial expressions.
- Take turns.
- Let him see your face when you are talking.
- Let him initiate communication.
- Read him books and magazines.
- Make it fun!

Language takes off
18 months to 3 years

Once your child has a vocabulary of around 30 words he will be able to start putting words together into two-word sentences. The two-word sentence may be simplistic but it is of great significance because it shows the child's desire — and ability — to communicate an original idea rather than just imitate adults. Words in these first sentences are usually sequenced in the correct order, but there will be words 'missing' compared with more sophisticated sentences. To understand what your child means, therefore, you often have to know the situation. When he says 'Daddy car', does he mean:

That's Daddy's car.
Let's go in Daddy's car.
Is that Daddy's car?
Daddy's gone in the car.

It may come as a surprise to see how much your child has already learned about language: in the above example, the possessive noun (Daddy) correctly precedes the noun which is owned (car).

Children are great copiers, and this skill is invaluable as your child learns more about talking. By using clear, short and easily understood sentences, you will provide a good model for sentence formation. Keep the speed steady and try not to lapse into fast chatter.

As we've already noted, a child's early sentences often sound like telegrams, with little words and grammatical markers omitted, as in 'ball in box'. Modelling will show him how to fill in the gaps.

Children often chatter to themselves or their toys. Whenever possible, this chatter should not be interrupted as interruptions usually cause the child to become self-conscious and stop. Chatting away to themselves is invaluable speaking practice which can aid the clarity of later speech.

Remember, it takes two to talk

Communication is a two-way interaction; it is made up of a series of turns. You take a turn to speak and then I take a turn to reply.

Right from the beginning when communicating with your baby, try to convey the message that you expect a response. Ask simple questions and pause for an answer. If there is no attempt to talk, repeat the question and after a short pause answer your own question simply:

'What do you want? (pause)
What do you want? (pause)
Do you want more juice? (pause) More?'

When he is talking, it is important that you pay attention; after all, you expect him to listen when you are talking. If you are busy talking all the time without giving him time to contribute, when will your child have the opportunity to practise his talking?

Create situations where your child can learn to take his turn. Helping with household chores and playing together are both good opportunities for your child to learn about turn-taking. Take turns stirring the cake or rolling the ball. At first your child may need to be prompted to take his turn.

Encourage eye contact when talking. You don't have to stare into each other's eyes! But looking at the person you are speaking to provides a positive communication environment and is an important skill to learn. Have you ever tried talking to someone who is constantly looking around them? Not only is it very disconcerting, but they seem to be indicating to you that they are not interested. That may be true, but it's more likely they just are not good at making eye contact.

When communicating is pleasurable for everyone concerned, frequency of speech will increase. You will have experienced this yourself. Everyone speaks more in a relaxed environment, with people they feel comfortable with.

When your young baby 'talks' back to you, cuddle and praise him for his communication. The tone of your voice and gleam in your eye will make him smile with pleasure.

When your child attempts any sort of talking, respond immediately, even if it's not very convenient. (You can always call from the top of the ladder!) Knowing that speech gets action from an adult is very satisfying. At the very least, praise the attempt: 'Good girl. Good talking. You want more.'

What about 'baby talk'?

Grandparents seem particularly fond of baby terms like 'dickie birds' and 'night nights'. Some parents feel that baby talk should be limited to the first nine months of life. Indeed, we would suggest there is no need to use baby talk at all. There seems little point or benefit in teaching words which have to be changed at a later date. This can be extremely difficult, especially for children with language problems.

Don't be put off by words which appear hard to say. 'Thank you' may come out as 'tang oo', but your intonation will be imitated as well and this will help you understand.

Your intonation, in fact, is very important. Many people naturally exaggerate their tone of voice and increase the use of facial expression and hand movements when they're talking to young children. If you are enthusiastic and entertaining, you will tend to hold your child's interest much longer. Don't

be afraid to exaggerate tonal and physical gestures when interacting with your child: 'Where are you?' with a rise and fall intonation and 'Thank you' with a fall intonation.

Quite often, in fact, intonation is learnt well before the words are mastered. Even though the words are impossible to understand in isolation, you will know from the tone that 'Air ar oo?' means 'Where are you?'.

Words that are spoken in an interesting manner are often learnt very quickly. It is not unusual for us to see children whose speech is generally unintelligible but who can articulate 'oh shit!' as clearly as can be!

Once your child can produce a simple sentence, he will see the value of communication and will rapidly learn more about using his language skills.

Language and knowledge are intimately mixed. His language will enable him to seek information, and this in turn will increase his language ability. A child will need language for his developing thoughts and this need will advance his talking. The more thinking he is doing, the more language he will develop. A child who is helped to use language well will use his potential for learning to good effect. His talking feeds his intelligence.

Beware of constantly criticising or pretending not to understand your child's talking unless it's on the advice of a speech pathologist. Your corrections may not have any effect other than to cause distress.

With a child under three years, there is no point in even correcting sounds. If you say 'No, it's not a tat', your confused child will think you are saying that it's not a cat — maybe it's a donkey or an elephant. He is trying to convey a message and you are creating confusion.

It is far more worthwhile to model the correct pronunciations by exaggerating the altered sounds — you make your point and give positive reinforcement at the same time: 'Yes, it's a *cat*'.

Moving on to more advanced concepts

Once your child's language ability begins to grow, he will be able to cope with concepts like counting and colours. The third part of this book talks about sources such as books, television and songs which are all very valuable in teaching these concepts.

Nursery rhymes are great for improving speech, not just through their subject matter but through rhyming, rhythm, gesture, inflection and sequencing. Rhythm and timing are essential for fluent, intelligible speech. What's more, rhymes are great fun and can make routine events like hair-washing enjoyable:

'This is the way we wash our hair, wash our hair, wash our hair . . .'

Counting can be encouraged throughout the day. How many times do you pour water on your child's hair to remove the soap? How many sandwiches? How many toes? How many wheels?

When has a word or concept been learnt? Be guided by your child. If he is getting bored and doesn't wish to

---

How to have great fun changing nappies

Daily chores are a great chance to help your child learn to talk and they can be made more fun with a little bit of imagination. Be relaxed with your child. Chat with him and enjoy his company — even if you are changing his nappy for the tenth time that day!

Here are some ideas for a speech lesson on the change table.

- Have a bright picture on the wall at your child's eye level, or a noisy toy. Draw his attention to it and tell him its name.

- Talk about the cloth you're using. 'Does it tickle your leg? Now I'm rubbing it on your arm.'

- Tickle his feet with the lotion bottle while you tell him what it is.

- Encourage him to copy you by blowing raspberries, poking out his tongue or making cooing sounds.

- Play peek-a-boo with a nappy, or hide a toy under the nappy.

- Give him some scrap paper to play with and tell him its name.

- Talk about his clothes. Can he throw his dirty clothes into the basket? Good shot!

Toddlers who are slower to talk

Although most children are producing recognisable words and simple sentences at around two years, some are not. This can cause considerable concern among parents, who see other children of the same age chatting away, and can also be increasingly frustrating for the toddler.

It's worth remembering that first words are related to your child's needs and interests; no child will talk unless there is a need to. If your child is the strong silent type, it may be that you are looking after him so well that you are anticipating all his needs and he has no call to talk. Try being a little less efficient! Give your child a chance to let you know he is thirsty.

If your child is old enough to look after himself by getting his own drink, it may be necessary to make life more inconvenient so that he needs to ask. When you're dealing with an independent toddler who insists on looking after himself, it may help to have a balance whereby he can get certain drinks on his own but needs to ask you to get others; have the juice in the door of the fridge so he can help himself but have the milk on the top shelf so he needs to ask for it.

This can be a useful strategy to convey the idea that you want him to talk and that speech is a useful tool for getting what he wants. Children want to convey messages, but they don't mind how they go about it. If pointing and grunting get the desired result, why should he have to say the word?

We are not advocating a stand up battle of wills. No matter what the age of your child there is no advantage in adding too much pressure and demanding speech. It does not help to refuse to cooperate with your child until he speaks — this can make him feel worried about communicating. If your child is not talking by two to two-and-a-half years, a speech pathologist will be able to offer specific advice.

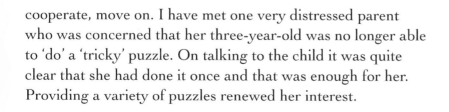

cooperate, move on. I have met one very distressed parent who was concerned that her three-year-old was no longer able to 'do' a 'tricky' puzzle. On talking to the child it was quite clear that she had done it once and that was enough for her. Providing a variety of puzzles renewed her interest.

Grasping grammar
3 to 5 years

What?

Why?

When?

How?

Childen

constantly ask

questions.

Although this way

may be wearisome,

it is how he learns

and how he

increases his

vocabulary.

By three years of age, the child's memory and forethought have developed so that he is no longer restricted to the 'here and now', but can often remember what happened yesterday and can plan for tomorrow. The three-year-old can talk about many things.

At the same time, his articulation has progressed to the point that he is now intelligible to strangers about 85 percent of the time, although he still makes some omissions or substitutions.

He is using nouns to name things, adjectives to describe them and verbs to tell you what they do. He is using 'ed' for the past tense 'dropped'. He is starting to slot in the small words between the main ones ('Daddy's car is in the garage'). He has some grasp of grammar ('a ball' and 'two balls'), although he will still make some errors ('me not want it').

He is constantly demanding to know 'what, why, when and how'. While this can be wearisome sometimes, it is how he learns and how he increases his vocabulary and other language skills.

At four years of age, a child's sentences are becoming more and more sophisticated, as are his thinking and indeed his play.

He still makes some grammatical errors, but some of these are, in fact, 'clever mistakes' which show that the child has learnt and can use the rules of his language. A sentence such as 'I swimmed over there' shows that he understands the rule for past tense: when we talk about something that has happened we put an 'ed' on the end. He has yet to learn that there are in fact exceptions to this rule!

Similarly, 'Look! Two mouses!' shows that he understands the rule for plural nouns: when there is more than one, we put an 's' on the end. Once again, he has yet to learn that in English there are exceptions to this rule. At a later stage, probably when he is at school, the child will learn that not all

At four years of age, a child's sentences are becoming more and more sophisticated, as are his thinking and indeed his play.

A sentence such as 'I swimmed over there' shows that he understands the rule for past tense.

Most children learn grammar — the rules of language — without anyone teaching them.

words follow the rules and will use irregular forms such as 'swam' and 'mice' correctly.

Indeed, most children learn grammar — the rules of language — without anyone teaching them. If your child has a significant problem, such as the words being in the incorrect order, or if he still speaks like a telegram at three years, then a full assessment will help clarify which areas need to be worked on.

However, if your child makes only occasional and common grammatical and language errors, the suggestions on the following page should help him to overcome them and at the same time expand his vocabulary. Many of these suggestions make use of modelling. Modelling can be used very effectively to correct speech sounds and grammar without making a fuss, and to expand vocabulary.

When your child says 'Him runs', you can reply 'Yes, he is running'. When he says 'Wa'er', you might say 'Yes, water. Here's the water'.

Helping to correct common mistakes

Plurals

If your child doesn't use plurals, such as 'two cars', try pairs memory games, matching to find more than one picture or object while saying 'one car . . . two cars!'.

'I' and 'me'

Some children use 'me' when they mean 'I', as in 'me do it'. This is a difficult one, because if you model the word 'me', the child is confused as to who you are talking about. The best way is to pick up his hand and pat his chest while modelling the sentence: 'I'll do that'.

Confusing genders

Some children don't differentiate between the two genders. Playing with dolls and dressing them up gives you the opportunity to model and practise: 'his pants, his hat, her bag, her chair'. You can also make pictures of things that are his or hers. Try looking at pictures or people and describing what they are doing: 'she is cooking', 'he is painting'. Exaggerate the words 'he' and 'she', then you can start encouraging him to use the correct words.

Similarly, your child might use the possessive when it's not required, as in 'her jumping over the rope'. Modelling and exaggerating the correct word is also helpful here.

'Doing'

Perhaps your child overuses this word, especially in response to a question: 'What's she doing?''She doing over a rope.'

The first step is to encourage use of the action word, in this case 'jumping'. Your child might then progress to saying 'She doing jumping over a rope'. Explain that he didn't have to say 'doing'. You can make a game of throwing the 'doing' into the rubbish bin. Point out also that you need the small word 'is': 'She is jumping over a rope'.

A hand signal can help to remind your child to use 'is'. Point out that it is such a little word and use your thumb and forefinger to indicate this. Use this signal each time you model the word.

Colours

Colours are often a sticking point for children. Try associating the colour with something in the environment and use this reference each time you name the colour: 'Your jumper is blue like the sky.' Others are 'yellow like the sun', 'green like the grass' and 'red like blood' (children always remember this one!).

Helping to correct common mistakes

Size

Contrasting sizes helps make the point to your children. Try not to restrict your child's use of concepts by always describing things as 'big' or 'little' — try using 'fat' or 'thin', 'long' or 'short', 'wide' or 'narrow'.

Prepositions

When modelling prepositions ('in, on, under, beside, behind, in front of'), work on only two at a time. For example, hide toys around the room: 'in' the box, 'under' the table, 'in' the doll's house, 'under' the chair.

Same and different

Picture pairs (a very useful game) can be used to point out when pictures are the same and when they are different. Some children have trouble with the concept of being different until it is shown as being 'not the same'.

Describing words

Try to expose your child to a variety of words. Rather than making yours too simple, remember to keep your language above your child's own skill level. If you describe your friend as 'good', how will he learn about 'funny', 'kind', 'happy', 'lively', 'cheerful' or 'helpful'?

Grouping words

Extend the range and grouping of words by asking your child to think of all the things he can wear, all the things he can ride on or in, or all the things he can eat. Maybe cut and paste posters of different word groups.

Sequencing

Draw a sequence of actions on different pieces of paper. For example, draw a child with nothing on, with his underwear on, with his underwear and jumper on, with his jumper and trousers on and with his jumper, trousers and shoes on, then ask your child to place them in the right order.

Speech sounds

At three, a large number of sounds are used but some may still be immature, with one sound substituted for another ('bish' for 'fish'). The three-year-old will rarely leave out sounds except when there are two consonants together, so he may still say 'boon' for 'spoon'.

From this age, sounds develop rapidly until five when all except for 'r', 'v' and 'th' are used correctly. A chart in the following section shows which sounds develop when.

Specific problems with sounds can be identified well before three. We see children for therapy who present as bright with good understanding, but who have difficulty producing sounds. One cute little two-year-old comes in each week, tugs on my sleeve and cheerfully says 'a oh'. Mum quickly follows on by saying 'hello'. He does not use any consonant sounds at all. Other children look as if talking takes a great deal of effort.

If you are concerned about your child's use of speech sounds, a speech therapist will be able to give specific advice, but again, there is much you can do yourself and 'sound play' can be great fun.

How can we have fun with sounds? Look at the boxes on pages 40–42 for some entertaining ways to teach your child how to make different sounds. Before your child can say a sound in a word, he needs to be able to say it on its own.

There are also plenty of games which you can play with your child to teach him about sounds, using objects or pictures which start with the target sound. Some of these games are described on these pages.

BINGO

Use two playing boards of pictures (one each) and collect matching small pictures of objects starting with the chosen sound. Each player places his playing board in front of him on the table. Place the small cards face down in a pile in the middle. The first player takes a card from the top of the pile and says the name of the picture on the card. He then places this card on the matching picture on his or your playing board. Players continue in turn. The first player to cover all the pictures on his board calls out 'Bingo!' and is declared the winner.

LUCKY DIP

Place the objects in a pillowcase or box. Your child can pick out one at a time and together you can practise naming it.

FISHING

Collect together pictures of objects with the chosen sound. Make a fishing rod with a stick, a piece of string and a magnet. Put paperclips on each picture and place the pictures in a box or bowl. Your child can name the pictures as he catches them.

PICTURE PAIRS

Cut out two pictures of objects starting with each of the chosen sounds. Place them face down on the table. Take it in turns to turn over two pictures, naming each one, until you find the matching pair.

CUTTING & PASTING

Make a special sound scrapbook.

HIDE 'N SEEK

Hide the objects around the room, and your child can name each one as he finds it.

SKITTLES

Stand the objects up like skittles. Roll a ball and name each object as you hit it.

WHAT'S MISSING?

Use objects or pictures and spread three or more face up in a row on the table in front of the child. The child says the name of the pictures in order from left to right. Then ask the child to close his eyes while you take one away. He has to name the missing one. If he does not guess it straight away, you might give him a clue.

How do we make
speech sounds?

You can help your child learn how to make sounds not only by saying them but by explaining what we do when we say them. Children learn more easily if we can use something to represent the sound. Exaggerate the sound when you say it. It may help him to watch your face as you make the sound.

Select a sound your child is able to copy and stick to that one for a short period of time. At this stage we are concerned with sounds only, so don't worry about the way words are spelt. For example, the sound 'k' is the initial sound in 'car', 'cat' and 'key', and the sound 's' is the initial sound in 'sand', 'circus' and 'celery'.

Here is a list of sounds and the way we make them.

m   The car says 'mmm'. Put your lips together and hum. Feel the vibrations on the side of your nose.

p   Make the candle flicker by saying 'p-p-p'. Put your lips together then quickly open them feeling the air on your hand.

b   The bouncing ball says 'b-b-b.' Put your lips together and then open them with a loud sound.

n   The jackhammer says 'nnn'. Put the tip of your tongue behind your top teeth and say 'no'. Feel the vibrations on the side of your nose.

w   The crying baby says 'w-w-w'. Put your lips forward as if you're about to whistle.

t   The dripping tap says 't-t-t'. Put the tip of your tongue up behind your top teeth and then let it drop down.

h   When the puppy dog pants he says 'h-h-h'. Open your mouth and puff on the back of your hand.

How do we make
speech sounds?

d   When we bang the drum we say 'd-d-d'. Put the tip of your tongue up behind your top teeth and make a loud sound as you drop your tongue down.

k   The shooting gun says 'k-k-k'. Open your mouth and pretend you're going to cough. Put your finger on your tongue to push it down and the back of the tongue will jump up to make the sound. If your child still finds this sound hard to produce, get him to practise gargling. This encourages the tongue into the right position.

g   The water going down the plughole says 'g-g-g'. Do the same as for 'k' but make a loud noise.

y   The yoyo says 'y-y-y'. Spread your lips out in a smile and put the tip of your tongue down behind your bottom teeth.

l   When we sing we say 'la-la-la'. Put the tip of your tongue up behind your top teeth and then drop it down. Do not use your lips.

f   The rabbit says 'fff' with his big front teeth. Bite your bottom lip with your top teeth and blow.

v   The aeroplane engine says 'vvv'. Do the same as for 'f' but make it a loud noise.

s   The snake says 'sss'. Put your teeth together, spread your lips in a smile and put the tip of your tongue up behind your top teeth.

z   The buzzing bee says 'zzz'. Do the same as for 's' but make a loud noise.

ch   The train says 'ch-ch-ch'. Put your teeth together, the tip of your tongue up behind your top teeth and make a loud explosion.

More speech sounds

sh   When we want someone to be quiet we say 'sh-sh'. Push your lips forward and do the same as for 's'.

r   The roaring lion says 'rrr'. Curl your tongue up in your mouth and smile.

th   Poke your tongue out between your teeth and blow.

Finetuning

From 5 years

By five years of age, your child will be talking almost as well as you. Certainly, his vocabulary will expand throughout his life, but he now knows most of the rules of our language and can use it appropriately.

Of course, once your child is talking fluently, stimulation shouldn't end. There is no substitute for time and conversation. Most of the techniques we have discussed are still relevant for the school age child. They are summarised here as a reminder.

- Continue talking to your child about what things are, where you find them and how they work.
- Take your discussions a stage further by working out alternatives and different possible outcomes.
- Once your child can read by himself, don't abandon those quiet times reading together. Try reading children's novels. There is a great variety available, and you can always seek advice from your local librarian.
- Practise what you preach: if your child sees you reading, he will be more inclined to enjoy books himself.
- Encourage your child to ask questions.
- Take the time to play with your child and enjoy his company.
- Listen carefully to his stories, as indeed you would like him to listen to yours.
- Find time to talk about your day. Make sure everyone has a turn. Be realistic — not every day is a good one but talking is an emotional outlet for everyone to discuss difficulties and ways of solving them.
- Reduce background noise during family conversation time.
- Monitor television viewing (see also chapter 3). Talk together about what you have seen.

Talking

Listening

Encouraging

Finding Time

Listen carefully to his stories, as indeed you would like him to listen to yours.

LEARNING *to* TALK, TALKING *to* LEARN

WHICH SOUNDS DEVELOP WHEN?

Sound	3	3 ½	4	4 ½	5	6	7
p	✖						
b	✖						
m	✖						
h	✖						
w	✖						
n	✖						
t	✖						
d	✖						
g	✖						
ng	✖						
y	✖						
k		✖					
f		✖					
l			✖				
sh			✖				
ch			✖				
s				✖			
z				✖			
j				✖			
r					✖		
v						✖	
th							✖

Around 75 percent of all children are correctly producing these sounds at the above ages.
Consonant blends (where two consonants occur together) such as 'swing', 'spoon' and 'blue' are mastered between four and six years.

'Articulation Development in Children Aged Three to Nine Years', Kilminster & Laird, in *Australian Journal of Human Communication Disorders*,1983.

~

CHAPTER THREE

LEARNING TO TALK FROM OTHER SOURCES

Other influences on a child's language development

Serious fun
The role of play

It has always been acknowledged that play is fun. However, until the beginning of this century it was also thought that play was a waste of time. It was accepted that young children spent their time playing because they were not capable of doing anything more useful. Once children went to school they were expected to work, and play was then kept for holidays or when work was completed. In actual fact, play *is* your child's work!

We now know that play is the most important activity in a child's life from birth through until about seven or eight years of age. Most of your baby's waking hours are spent at play. Your young child learns just about everything through play. Play is necessary to an infant's physical, social and language development. It is more than just a means of passing time or keeping children occupied. Watching your child at play is really watching your child work. He can explore himself and the world around him. He can practise old skills and develop new ones. How can this hard work be called 'just playing'?

Playing comes naturally to most children. As adults, we need to remind ourselves that the many hours spent in playing are really laying the foundation for all intellectual activity. Free play has an important role but as adults we must also remember that we can help our child to realise his full learning potential by modifying and developing play activities.

Most children want to learn to talk and later to read and write, and many of the toys they play with at an earlier age help them do this. There is no question that children who have had good play opportunities and a wide variety of play experiences will have an obvious advantage when learning to talk, read and write.

What can play do?

- Play has many purposes for a young child. It is a serious business which should never be frowned upon by adults.

- Play allows your child to develop new skills through observation, exploration and discovery.

- Play allows your child to practise skills he has already learned.

- Play develops language understanding, concept formation and language expression. Children seldom play silently, even when alone. They are constantly talking. It gives them practice in conveying, reporting and discovering information. It can be used to describe incidents and tell stories. Play enables questions to be asked.

- Play is fun.

- Play can relieve boredom and frustration and allow for the release of physical energy.

- Play can let your child experience and express feelings of achievement, failure, satisfaction, pleasure and frustration.

- Play allows your child to act out other people's roles and help develop a sex role identity.

- Play helps children form friendships and gain cooperation. It also allows your child to learn how to cope with himself and other people.

- Play allows your child to be creative and independent. The level of creativity and discovery will invariably match the child's environment.

What different ways do children play?

If you watch your child as he grows, you will see that his play changes. As the child becomes more skilled and experienced his play becomes more creative, diverse and sophisticated.

EXPLORATORY PLAY

Exploratory play, which begins at about three months, lets your child observe and discover objects in his environment. Objects arouse curiosity and a desire to learn and your child will use all his senses to find out about them. He can touch, taste, smell, look at and listen to the object. Finger play is important for eye–hand coordination, seeing where sounds come from, under-standing the permanence of objects and learning to appreciate time and space. Try playing 'This Little Piggy Went to Market' and 'Round and Round the Garden' with your child's fingers or toes.

IMITATIVE PLAY

This type of play begins at about nine months and reflects what your child sees and hears around him, particularly in everyday situations. Toddlers love to imitate their parents and need continued opportunity to observe 'models'. By providing them with safe and similar replicas of the object you use, you can let them participate in seemingly mundane chores in an enjoyable way. You are setting the scene for them to learn how to carry out certain actions, and later why to carry out these actions.

ACTIVE PLAY

Let's get physical! This type of play helps your child's physical development. He will learn to control his body better and coordinate his movements. Once independent, he is free to explore the world around him. So, let your child crawl, roll, jump, climb so long as it's safe.

CONSTRUCTIVE PLAY

Constructive play begins at 18 months and enables your child to participate in an activity which results in an end product, such as building a tower with blocks. It is important for developing eye–hand coordination and memory. This type of play provides the perfect opportunity for learning about the size, shape, texture, weight and colour of objects.

IMAGINATIVE AND MAKE-BELIEVE PLAY

In this type of play children will use objects or gestures to represent other objects or events that are not present. Imaginative play is full of make-believe, fantasy and role-play. It is of vital importance in language and social development. 'Let's pretend' games prepare your child for the many situations and relationships he will encounter later on. Values and attitudes are developed through fantasy play also.

Role-playing helps your child learn to understand others. If he is to understand others, he must have the chance to put himself in another's place.

Imaginative play also encourages

LEARNING *to* TALK, TALKING *to* LEARN

creativity. The richer your child's environment, the more experiences he will have to act out. It allows your child freedom to make his own choices. The growing complexity of play at this stage signals your child's increased capacity to think and use language. More complex thinking means more complex play and vice versa.

GAMES WITH RULES

To play games with rules, your child needs to be able to share and take turns. He must also be able to follow instructions and discuss the outcome of the game. Such games allow your child to practise language skills, and learn the social skills of winning and losing.

Using toys to teach talking

When buying, choosing or making a toy, think about your child's level of language. How many words can he say? Is he at the single word or three-word phrase level? Look at the particular toy and think about what words you could model and encourage your child to copy whilst playing with it.

Let's look at a few toys and see what words you could teach.

BUILDING BLOCKS

- Blocks can represent many things such as people, cars, trains.
- Blocks can be used to teach numbers, colour and shape concepts.
- Specific words to practise include numbers, colours, same and different.
- Other words to model include 'more', 'on top', 'fall down', 'up', and 'down'.

PUZZLES

- Children love doing puzzles over and over and therefore you have lots of scope for teaching new words.
- Ask your child 'Where's . . .?'.
- Child asks for more when he's ready to fit another piece.
- Other words to model include here and there, in there and in the hole.
- Hold up a choice of two pieces and your child names the one he wants next.

BUBBLE BLOWING

- This is a cheap and fun activity.
- Incorporate words such as 'more', 'pop', 'all gone', 'bubbles' and 'no more'.

Remember, always talk with your child when playing together and give your child time to respond and talk!

Who needs toys?

Toys are not always necessary and you can have just as much fun playing without them. Remember also that toys do not have to have been bought from a shop. And art activities don't have to be put on hold until kindergarten. Most things you need you probably already have at home. Don't throw anything out! Here are some suggestions for play without toys.

NEWBORN

- Hold him close in front of you so he can look straight at you. Rock him gently.

- Have a conversation with him by taking turns with you by slightly nodding his head, moving his eyes and mouth.

0 TO 6 MONTHS

- Encourage him to copy you blowing bubbles or blinking deliberately. He may even make noises as if he's talking back to you.

- Hide a toy he's been following and then ask 'Where's it gone?' Make it re-appear and say 'There it is'.

- Have a mobile and some hitting toys around. Cotton reels, silver foil and ribbons blow well in the breeze.

- Play 'Peep-bo'.

- Let him touch you and pull your hair. Tickle him.

- Encourage him to splash in the bath and swim, if he likes it.

6 TO 9 MONTHS

- Vary physical games from being held under the arms and gently swung, to clapping hands and a noisy rough-and-tumble.

- Use sound makers such as rice in pots as rattles or rollers. Have things to bang.

- Play 'Pat-a-cake'.

- Let baby grasp your fingers as you move and sing 'Row the boat'.

- Play 'Round and round the garden' and 'This little piggy'.

- Let him copy you building towers — use yoghurt pots — and of course making them fall down.

9 TO 12 MONTHS

- Let him try out new ways of moving, such as riding in a supermarket trolley.

- Continue bathtime fun.

- Play action rhymes.

- Encourage him to copy you by smacking his lips, waving, clapping and banging hands on a table.

- Stare at his reflection in a mirror, or offer it a toy.

- Start off a game of 'Peep-bo' by hiding.

- Initiate games where he offers things to you and you give them back.

- Crawl around together during exploring games.

12 to 18 months

- Encourage him to copy you (washing up) and help you (sweeping the floor). Use a real dustpan and a real telephone. Telephone companies often give away old telephones, so it's worth making some enquiries.

- Make games out of routines such as getting dressed, or putting away the shopping. 'How many hands? One, two. Where are your hands? There they are!'

- Hide objects around the room and find them together.

- Play 'Ring-a-ring-'o-roses' and musical chairs.

- Play in the playground in the park. Feed the ducks, jump in a pile of leaves.

- Put together homemade books including a 'Me Book' about your child's activities, family and friends.

2 TO 3 YEARS

- Encourage messy play.

- Play 'hide 'n seek'.

- Use sand and water for playing with sieves and old cartons.

- Playdough is good for squeezing. Biscuit cutters can be used to make different shapes.

- Play pretend games with dolls and teddies, using real plastic cups and an old jug, and improvising furniture, such as a box for a bed.

- Make a collage from shells, feathers and leaves collected on a walk and stuck on a piece of paper.

- Build a cubby house by using a big blanket over a table and hanging down the sides.

- A small box or a couple of bricks can be used to jump on and off.

- A plank resting on two bricks is good to walk along.

- Create a fishing game with corks, paper clips, rods and a magnet.

- Use old plastic cartons for skittles and roll a ball to knock them down.

- Line up chairs, facing the same way, to make cars or trains.

- Use a sock to make a puppet.

- Body painting is fun — draw around your child's body and cut the paper into pieces. Makes a great puzzle!

3 TO 4 YEARS

- Thread coloured macaroni onto a piece of string to make a necklace.

- Playdough can be used in more sophisticated ways.

- Different buttons and lids can be sorted into empty ice cream containers.

- Make a sewing card. Draw a picture on a piece of card. Make holes with a needle every 2 cm. The child can use a large needle and wool to 'sew' the card.

- Imaginative play can be more sophisticated.

The rhythm section
The role of music and other sounds

Music and rhythm are part of our environment. You needn't have belonged to the school choir to enjoy bopping along to the Top 40 hits. Your children won't mind if you sing out of tune, so long as you can share the pleasures of music with them. The listening skills that children learn through musical activities can help their whole development. After all, just about every activity at school depends on listening. The creative side of music becomes a useful tool for expression and once again links the child with his environment.

Children learn to respond to music very early and soon begin to involve themselves, even before they are born. Many women experience their babies responding to music at some stage during pregnancy. One of our children was always soothed and comforted by a violin concerto but would give a violent kick to jazz!

This quietening and sudden reaction can also be observed in the very young baby. Soon he starts moving his body and swaying and later he copies rhythm and sounds. Initially you will provide the music and words and help your child do the actions. Then, after many repetitions, encourage your child to take an active part if he is not already doing so spontaneously. It may seem obvious that body coordination and physical development will benefit from musical activities.

Music activities for your child are easy to organise. All you need is the two of you and your voices! You can make music in the car, in the bath, in the park, anywhere! Music activities are great for your child's language development because they can include:

- vocal play;
- actions as well as talking;
- physical contact;
- repetition;
- turn taking;
- non-verbal responses.

Listening

Responding

Singing

Enjoying

Learning

The listening skills that children learn through musical activities can help their whole development.

Children learn to respond to music very early.

Music activities for your child are easy to organise. All you need is the two of you and your voices!

One of the most important things children learn from musical and other sound activities is sound awareness. Your child may have perfect hearing but he needs to understand and respond to what he hears. Let him listen to all kinds of sounds: personal (sneezing), environmental (tap running), lullabies, marches, instrumental, orchestral music. By doing this you are helping your child to respond appropriately to different sounds. Every day we react to many sounds in our environment: the car screeching, sirens going, the school bell ringing in the morning. Attentive listening helps your child notice different speech sounds such as the quiet 't' sound, the louder 'd' sound and the long 's' sound. The box at the end of this section gives other suggestions for activities based on sound.

Listening also helps your child learn to associate words and actions. Nursery rhymes, action rhymes and finger games are useful for teaching your child to pay attention. If you exaggerate the rhyme and leave pauses, your child will learn to anticipate. In 'Humpty Dumpty', for example, you will find he is leaning over before you have even said the words 'and had a great fall'.

As your child gets older you can replace the key word and make it more stimulating. Most two- to two-and-a-half year olds find it great fun if you sing 'Baa baa black cow'. See if they can spot the mistake!

Try to keep rhymes brief and interesting. Make the actions near your face to encourage the child to look at your lips, eyes and hands. Play finger games where you touch some part of his body. 'Incy Wincy Spider', 'This Little Piggy', and 'Open, Shut Them' are all good for this. Action songs are good for teaching turn-taking and imitation. Such songs include 'Ring-a-Ring-'o Roses', 'Row, Row, Row Your Boat', 'The Wheels of the Bus', and 'Johnny Works with One Hammer'.

Using rhymes is a very good way to extend memory and even aid learning. With the *Sesame Street* 'Alphabet Song', your child will remember the tune and rhythm well before he learns the letters. (You'll remember from an earlier chapter that even when you are just talking, children will copy the rhythm of the talking first. A child who is used to hearing you say 'Where are you?' will often be able to say 'Air ar oo?' with the rise and fall of your voice copied perfectly long before he can pronounce the words correctly.)

Rhythm can also help children learn to spell, especially longer words. Most of us learned to count by using some rhythmical pattern such as number tables.

Music can make daily routines and difficult times easier for your child and for yourself. For example, if he needs to walk some distance, make up a song about 'walking in the city'. You could do the same for activities such as washing his hair and sitting on the potty.

Rhythm instruments such as drums can be used to express feelings:

'How does this boy feel?'
'He's angry.'
'Let's play the drum in an angry way.'

Many language concepts can be taught through music. Your child can run fast or slow to the music. He can dance on tip-toe for high notes and on the ground for low notes. He might love to stamp his feet for loud sounds and creep for soft quiet sounds. Can he pick out long notes and short notes? Colours could also be taught by having instruments colour coded.

As your child gets older, music can be linked to stories and poetry. A story such as *The Three Bears* could be used. Make musical sounds for different parts of the story and include a variety of rhythm patterns and pitch and speech patterns. Other stories to try are *The Gingerbread Man, Puff the Magic Dragon, Rudolf the Red-Nosed Reindeer* and *The Three Billy Goats Gruff.* For more ideas, see Appendix I — the Children's booklist.

Songs are often poems that have been set to tunes. Your child will enjoy making up his own tune for a verse. Once he is old enough to be more aware of speech sounds, experiment with both vowel and consonant sounds. Can he change the pitch and volume as he says 'm' and 'ah'?

One of the most important aspects of using music with a toddler is that it is enjoyable for both of you. You do not have to be a trained opera singer to sing and have fun with your child! Many children love using a tape recorder and this is an ideal way to pass some of the hours when driving long distances or flying somewhere. Remember not to exclude all conversation.

Remember too that children do grow tired of or outgrow songs so always keep on the lookout for new ones. There are many cassettes available for young children, with the *ABC for Kids* series with Peter Combe and Don Spencer amongst the most popular ones.

Older children may like to use a walkman sometimes, which means you can listen to your own music! Check your toy library or local council library regularly for any new tapes. Listen to them with your child and have fun!

Sound play

- Teach your child 'Old Macdonald Had a Farm'. You can have great fun pretending to be different animals and making their noises. You might also make a mobile of animals either drawn or cut from magazines. Your child will be able to discover the sound of paper crinkling and the sound of crayons on paper, too.

- Repeat patterns of claps using three to five beats of varying speed and volume.

- Ask your child to run around the garden, only stopping when you blow a whistle. How quickly can he respond?

- Use household items like pots, bowls and shoe boxes as drums. They will all give a different tone.

- Have your child choose which instrument is being played from items such as a bottle shaker and bell.

- Ask your child to decide whether you are clapping, knocking or beating. Is it loud or soft?

- Make different voices — happy, sad and loud ones, high pitched and low pitched ones.

- Draw teddies with different faces — sad, happy, surprised, tired. Ask your child to match the voice to the face.

- Find the hidden music box. Play the child's music box hidden under a blanket or furniture. See if he can find where the music is coming from.

- Dramatise a character or object such as a tree standing with its branches reaching high into the sky, or a snake slithering low on the ground.

- Use television programs like *Playschool* and *Fat Cat* as sources of ideas for musical activities.

- Expose your child to different types of music — jazz, classical, pop, and so on.

- Sing favourite nursery rhymes or songs. Perhaps change some of the words.

- Dance to music. Encourage different actions to match the changes in music e.g. scurry like mice, stand like giants, fly like aeroplanes.

- You and your child can clap to music, altering the speed and volume as appropriate.

- Make up songs to familiar melodies.

- Make up games with rhyming words. 'What do you hit a ball with that rhymes with (sounds like) bat?'

- Whisper speech sounds.

- Bang out names and messages, with one beat for each syllable — gar-den, An-na-bel.

- Musical Bumps, or Stop the the Whistle. These two games work in opposite ways. In the first, your child jumps up and down to the music but must sit down quickly when the music stops. The latter game requires only a whistle. Let your children run around the garden until you blow the whistle. How quickly can they respond?

Read any good books lately?

Why should we write about books? How will this help your child to talk? Quite simply, books provide almost unlimited possibilities for learning not only about the world but also about how to use language.

Reading books together is an excellent activity which stimulates your child's talking and provides a foundation of pre-reading skills.

A child can enjoy and benefit from being read to right from birth. Keep a selection of books within easy reach and make a practice of showing them to him early, even from the day you first bring him home. Why not snuggle up on the sofa with your newborn and share the delights of your magazine? It doesn't have to be a baby book. Your baby will enjoy the physical contact and listening to your voice as you read to him.

It is good to also have some special baby books. Uncluttered books with bright primary colours are often more attractive to your child than the books illustrated in subtle colours which seem to be more attractive to adults.

Your baby will probably want to grab the book — this is his way of telling you he is interested. You'll be astonished at how early he may give signs of knowing which book he is looking at.

As your baby becomes more mobile, he will want to be physically active even when reading. Use rhythm and actions — when reading 'Humpty Dumpty', pretend to fall with your child at the appropriate time. Tickle or cuddle at a particular point and you'll find that your baby begins to anticipate it, if you give him time. Even by six months he may become excited when he recognises a picture of a familiar person or toy.

Wordless picture books can open doors to your baby's imagination. Books by Dick Bruna and the *First Picture Books* in the Ladybird series are good examples. There is a wide range of books on the market suitable for babies. Rag and

Books provide almost unlimited possibilities for learning not only about the world but also about how to use language.

A child can enjoy and benefit from being read to right from birth.

By 18 months he will want his favourite stories read again and again. You may be bored with the constant repetition but he will be delighted.

board books are a matter of taste — be guided by your child as some children just don't respond to them. There are also many bath books available. Many children enjoy homemade scrapbooks or photographs of themselves and their family, so keep a book of old Christmas and birthday cards handy for these times, too.

Remember that if you decide on ordinary paper books, they may not be kept in pristine condition. If the child has learnt from the book, does it matter if it is dog-eared and has pages repaired with sticky tape?

Books of nursery rhymes are also good to introduce at any time. They are popular with even the youngest children because of their catchy phrasing. Intonation and rhythm become more meaningful, and through having nursery rhymes read over and over the child will eventually come to recognise the words. Memorising plays an important part in early reading. Tickling games and finger play with repetitive lines are loved by all children for the same reasons.

As your baby grows, try to find the time to read to him, little and often. Choose a peaceful time when neither of you is too tired. Let your baby see the book and give him time to look at the pictures and respond. It will be more fun if you choose books that you and your child can both enjoy.

As he gets older, constant repetition of favourite stories will give your child an intuitive feeling about the patterns and structures of language. By the time he is 18 months old, *you* may be bored by the constant repetition of the same story but he will be delighted. He will also love stories with repetitive lines, like 'Who sank the boat?' each time you turn the page. Reading aloud is an excellent turn-taking activity — if you pause, your child can fill in the words.

One of the aims of reading to your child is to provide language that he can imitate at some later time. It will also stimulate him to both give and receive some simple information about the book you're looking at. Your child's contribution will depend on his level of language development. Your response can provide him with a model or prompt for a greater contribution. For example, if he just says 'Thomas', you might say:

'Look at naughty Thomas! What's going to happen?'

Books and your baby

- Learning to read will be easier if your child is used to looking at books.

- Books are a good source of topics to talk about.

- Reading to your baby encourages him to listen.

- Start with simple, brightly coloured books.

- Make looking at books a regular part of each day.

- Point out to your child that there are other things to read beside books.

- Use the library.

Welcome any observation about the pictures.

Three-year-olds like books that tell a story and have an ending that makes sense. Books can be used to help your young child understand and cope with new situations and feelings such as going to hospital or the arrival of a new baby.

Making a book is one of the simplest ways of encouraging a child to become a storyteller. The child creates his own original works featuring himself and other close people. With help a child of three can make 'What I did today' books. His little sentences become books once you write them down; the children draw pictures or you use photographs and then give the pages a cover. Easy access to crayons will encourage your child to scribble, draw and write. This is a great way to increase a child's confidence.

Continuing to use conversational strategies with children of four and older will stimulate their language and thinking skills. Try to use what you have been reading about as a starting point for discussing the child's own past or anticipated experiences and feelings: if reading *Thomas the Tank Engine*, you might remind him of his visit to the train museum.

Reading to your child does not have to be limited to books. Encourage an interest in everything from labels to signs, brochures, menus, words that flash up in television commercials. A child learns early that print representations stand for objects. In fact they learn this before you expect them to. For example, young children know that yellow arches signify McDonald's and STOP on a hexagonal red and white sign means you don't go on.

Read-and-talk time

Books are a perfect example of how learning to talk ties in with talking to learn. Whether you are reading aloud to your child or whether he is just looking at the pictures, talking should be part of the activity. Some writers refer to this as 'read-and-talk time'. You can talk before reading, during reading and after reading.

As soon as you show your child the cover of the book and tell him the title, his imagination will start to work. Set the scene by giving a one-sentence summary of the story and perhaps asking a key question.

A favourite story of ours is *My Hippopotamus Is On Our Caravan Roof Getting Sunburnt* by Hazel Edwards. When reading this book, you might say:

'This is about a hippopotamus who goes to the beach for a holiday with the little girl's family.'

Then you could add:

'You've been to the beach. Did we take a hippopotamus on our holiday?'

Any child we've read this book to is already bursting with questions before

Books and your pre-school child

- Books help develop a child's concentration and attention span.

- Parents' natural responses (imitating, labelling, expanding, promoting and repetition) are all part of sharing a book and developing language.

- Books help develop a vocabulary and verbal skills.

- Parents can initiate specific learning by choosing specific books.

- Books help develop thinking and imagination.

- Children will enjoy the stories and want to learn to read.

- Books help to develop awareness of specific concepts related to reading, for instance following the text from left to right, and from top to bottom.

- It can be very useful to take a book for your child while you are:

  in a waiting room,

  on a bus or train,

  having a lunch break when shopping,

  waiting in a shop.

we've even started reading. You can answer some questions, but then suggest:

'Let's read the story to see what happens.'

When children look at a book such as *My Hippopotamus* . . . the first thing that grabs their attention is the pictures: 'Wow! Look at that hippo eating cake!'

We have shared this book with the same children many times and on occasions don't read any of the text. The pictures are enough to spark off a story and conversation between the reader and the child.

Whether your four-year-old wants you to read or your two-year-old just wants to look at and talk about the pictures, you can still stir up the imagination. Ask questions like:

'What will happen if the hippo doesn't put his floatie on?'
'Why is the hippo wearing sunglasses?'

Ask your child who he knows who wears sunglasses.

Stories are also a good way to talk about your child's feelings. Help him to relate the feelings of the characters to his own everyday experiences:

'How did you feel when you caught a fish with Daddy at the beach?'
'Do the mum and dad look tired?'
'What does Daddy like to do when he's tired?'

Explain causes and effects and see if your child can guess what might happen on the next page:

'Will the hippo go shell hunting?'

There are endless dialogues that can go on between you and your child when reading a book together. It is these dialogues which will stimulate your child's language and stretch his thinking.

When are children ready to learn to read?

Traditionally children begin to learn to read on starting school. Many children, in fact, are ready before this time. However, there's no need to teach your pre-schooler to read in a formal way. As with talking, your child will learn a great deal about reading from watching you.

As we have already discussed, one of the major ways children learn anything is through imitation. They not only imitate sounds but also the actions of adults and older children, so if they see people around them reading and experiencing books, they will follow that example. By watching you, your child will learn how books work; that is, you start at the beginning and turn the pages over to work your way to the back of the book. As he watches you run your finger under the text, he will realise that the words on the page have meaning and that we work through the sequence from left to right.

Keep his books within easy reach and your child will eventually sort through them and 'read' them alone, or initiate the activity by bringing the book to you.

As your child gets older, choose books you both enjoy. If you find the story boring it is difficult to read it with enthusiasm, and enthusiasm is important in encouraging him to eventually enjoy reading himself. There will be times when your child will want the same book over and over again. Perhaps this is a good time to take turns — your child chooses one book, you choose the next.

Early beginner books stress word recognition through repetition. Reading is not a matter of recognising words first and then getting the meaning, but rather the meaning guides and aids the recognition of words.

Books are not the only tool to use in helping your child learn to read. Although learning to read can be quite repetitious, there are all sorts of games which can take the boredom out of the repetition and some of these are described on the next few pages.

It is preferable to use lower case letters when writing, not capital letters. Make use of phonics, where we use the letter's sound rather than its name: 'a' as in 'apple'. The list on page 71 gives a full alphabet of phonics.

A child learns to read in the same sequence as he learns to speak: sounds (letters), then words, and finally sentences.

Family Names

Make name cards for each member of the family, including visitors such as grandparents, and pets.

a) Before a meal, place each card at the appropriate place at the dinner table.

b) Draw family members and find the appropriate name cards to go with the drawings.

c) Muddle all the cards together. Work out what each card says and give it to the person. Perhaps stick it to their foreheads? They look very silly and that's part of the fun.

d) Musical hats — pin a name card to a hat. Pass around the hat when the music is playing. When the music stops, the person holding the hat has to read the card and place it on the appropriate person's head.

Labels

Make two sets of cards for different items in the room. First, stick the labels on each item, then give the matching card to your child and see if he can find it.

After a while, take the labels down. Muddle them up and help your child read them and stick them back in the appropriate places. If he gets it wrong, make a joke of it:

'Oh-oh! He's put the word "bed" on the door.'

Lean against the door and pretend to go to sleep. Have fun!

It's a good idea to make a habit of labelling windows, doors, cupboards and favourite toys around the house. Simply print the word on a piece of card and attach it to the object. Leave notes in lunch boxes and around the house. Use a wide vocabulary: children learn the shapes as well as the sounds of words. It also encourages guessing in context which is a valuable reading skill.

Post Boxes

Make two boxes with slits to post 'letters'. Write a letter onto two cards and stick one onto each box. On some old envelopes, write some simple words which begin with the same letters as on the boxes. Give one box to teddy and the

other to rabbit. Pretend to be a postman with a bag full of letters. Check each envelope to see if the first letter is the same as on the box. If it is, post it.

Sound Scrap Book

When learning a new letter, write it in a scrap book. Cut out pictures of objects starting with the letter and paste them into the book. Your child will love this activity, especially if you are not too fussy about neatness!

Letter Skittles

Use empty plastic bottles or skittles. Put a different letter on each skittle.

Take turns in throwing the ball. Name the letter knocked over and ask:

'Can you think of a word beginning with that sound?'

I Spy

An old favourite! 'I spy with my little eye something beginning with . . .' Choose the sound and ask others to guess what you can see.

Phrases and Sentences

Write down some action words on cards, such as 'hopping', 'tickling' and 'jumping'. Read them together and carry out the activity. This can be taken one step further by using the name cards as well, to make phrases like 'Mummy jumping'. Children love seeing their parents make fools of themselves! As your child becomes familiar with individual words, you can start putting more of them together. Use your cards to make simple, fun sentences like 'Mummy is tickling Sarah', then carry out the action.

A Few Other Ideas

Point out words when you are out shopping, such as 'Push' and 'Pull' on the doors.

When your child draws a picture, write a couple of words on it to describe what is happening.

With our busy lives today it is often easier to put on the television than to think of a more interesting, more stimulating activity. Sometimes we need to remind ourselves of the benefit of talking to, playing with and providing books for our children.

Through the enjoyment of books your children will learn to value your company and develop a greater appreciation and understanding of language.

The children's booklist in Appendix I gives plenty of suggestions for children of all ages.

SOUNDS

a	apple
b	bed
c	cat
d	dog
e	egg
f	fish
g	gate
h	hand
i	inside
j	jug
k	key
l	leaf
m	moon
n	nose
o	orange
p	pig
q	queen
r	rabbit
s	sun
t	tap
u	up
v	violin
w	window
x	axe
y	yawn
z	zip

Television Viewing

In 1990, the Australian Children's Television Foundation estimated that a million children watched approximately 23 hours of television every week, with pre-schoolers averaging 30 hours. This is more time for watching television than for any other activity except sleeping, and as much time as some students spend getting a university degree.

Rounded individuals or square eyes?

The role of television

Television viewing has advantages and disadvantages. Television can be watched for entertainment and information. There is nothing wrong with watching just for entertainment; not all television viewing needs to be educational.

Precisely because it is a tool for entertainment, education and information, television can play a constructive part in a child's life. The years of highest television viewing are often between the ages of two and four, and these years coincide with a critical time in the development of language, imagination and many other skills. Thus, a child who spends much of his day watching television is missing out on practising skills such as running, playing, looking at books and, very importantly, talking.

Carmen Luke, in her book *TV and Your Child*, says: 'Cumulative television hours — say, three to five hours of unmediated daily viewing — over the first four to five years in the child's life may impede the development of manual dexterity, as well as other social and verbal skills, at a crucial developmental stage.'

Television is a powerful teacher, and what it teaches may be good or bad. Let's look first at the good side. Used wisely, television can certainly have many advantages. Substantial research shows that appropriate television viewing can enhance play and creativity. Many young children tend to play and watch television at the same time; television may stimulate play ideas and even pretend characters.

Television can also help increase your child's vocabulary and be the starting point for language-building activities. Your presence and participation gives your child greater opportunity to express thoughts and feelings. It can help your child retain information because you can sing along and repeat words later and even draw pictures, letters and numbers when the program is finished.

Television is a powerful teacher. It can be a starting point for language building activities. But a child who spends too much of his day watching television is missing out on practising skills such as running, playing, looking at books and, very importantly, talking.

If you know what your child has watched, you can have the child re-tell the story as a bedtime story or you can re-tell the story together and practise turn-taking skills. If you are actively participating in the viewing, you will know if your child uses what he has seen and heard constructively in other activities.

You can discuss the program contents as well as its positive and negative aspects during and after viewing. Home video recorders allow you to record, review and discuss programs together. Studies show that by discussing a program with your child you can increase the benefits and reduce any negative effects. It gives you the opportunity to explain the meaning of new words and to clarify controversial scenes.

Television can help with the learning of language concepts, especially the more abstract concepts of time and space: Big Bird playing hide and seek in *Sesame Street*. It is the strong visual component which aids this learning. Watching a program with your child can set the scene for another hour of fun play afterwards. If they had been talking about position concepts during the program, you could then go off with your child and make an obstacle course relating it to the activities you have viewed.

Watching television can relax and soothe young children as well as exciting and stimulating them. Most toddlers like to watch television for a short period each day and it can be a useful and pleasant pastime. After the child has been busily playing, he enjoys just sitting and watching a suitable program.

On the bad side, as well as excluding the child from other activites, as already mentioned, too much television viewing can restrict the development of more complex language skills. Many programs contain sentences that are simple in form and therefore do not provide the opportunity to extend the child's existing language structures. Listen to the program and ask yourself: 'Is this how I want my child to talk?'

Television programs should be appropriate and match your child's level of understanding and life experiences.

Also, be aware of commercials played during children's viewing times — they may cause more headaches than the program. The fast and often complex verbal messages used may not be understood by your child, which can lead to tears

Guidelines for television viewing

- Keep television viewing as a positive activity right from the beginning. Encourage particular programs and know what your child is watching.

- Help your child understand why he is watching television. This will encourage him to be active, and by using more cognitive effort he will learn to become more critical in viewing and thinking.

- Don't leave the television on as background noise. It may discourage conversation. Encourage your child to turn it off if he is not interested.

- If your baby or toddler watches television from a restricted place, such as a high chair, there is no alternative but to watch. If children are on the floor or in baby walkers they at least have the chance to move away when they want to. This will help them learn to watch and listen more selectively.

- Young children like having the volume switched up high but check that it's not too loud. It can damage their hearing.

- Try to watch the television with your child if you can. This will make it easier to lead the conversation towards what the show is about, maybe about an unusual character or specific words that are used. Ask questions and encourage your child to make comments. Even with very young children, you can encourage and increase their attention span as well as helping them follow actions.

- Some parents report that television triggers 'bad' habits such as thumb-sucking. If such habits do occur, closer supervision is certainly required whilst the child is watching television.

- Television programs can interfere with family times. How often have you seen meals delayed whilst waiting for a favourite program to finish? Meal times are one of the most important times for a child to practise his developing communication skills. Sitting at a table without the interruption of television is also desirable if the child is to learn the manual skills of eating and also table manners. He needs to watch the model of other family members and cannot do that if he or they are watching television at the same time. Video recorders can help here by taping a favourite program to watch at a more suitable time.

- Be careful of advertising which can indoctrinate very young children about junk foods, toys and behaviour.

later; if all the child understood was that it was a 'big car' but not that it required batteries and a special track to operate on, he cannot understand why you won't buy it for him!

As well as exposure to what may be considered unrealistic values, exposure to violence is one of the most pervasive concerns about television watching for young children. Studies have pointed out that by their mid-teens children will have seen tens of thousands of violent incidents and thousands of deaths. These will have been portrayed in both cartoon and realistic form and will have been screened in so-called 'children's viewing hours'. For children, indirect experiences seen on television can be just as powerful as real personal experiences.

Television can become a part of their daily routine for many children from the age of three months. How many mothers do you know who turn on the television every day when they sit down to feed their baby? It doesn't take long for this to become a daily ritual.

Think about what your child might be doing if he wasn't glued to the screen. Is he missing out on learning other important things? What about time for talking, reading, playing, walking and jumping?

Television should never be a substitute for reading. In fact there is no substitute for reading! Children who see their parents use television as the main means of entertainment, rather than reading, may not be as willing to look at books.

Your child would be far better out in the fresh air on a summer's day getting exercise by running, jumping or playing with the dog rather than being cooped up in the air-conditioned family room watching cartoons! You are more likely to see your child with that spaced-out stare in front of the television than when he's racing his Matchbox cars up and down the pathway.

Playing and talking with you or a friend provide many more opportunities for active interaction than sitting in front of the television.

Whilst television can help your child learn, it should never replace — can never replace — conversation or reading aloud as the best stimulation for language development.

Are you panicking that your child watches too much television? Relax! We are not anti-television. We have all been guilty of using *Playschool* as a babysitter whilst we get on with other chores. We are just suggesting that television can play a more constructive part in your family life.

So, what should your child watch? It is wise to adopt the approach of moderate and balanced viewing of a variety of programs. Spend some time with your child watching programs and make a choice together.

What are our opinions on children's programs such as *Sesame Street* and *Playschool*? *Sesame Street* does create a fast pace with rapid jumps from one thing to another. In contrast, *Playschool* goes at a much slower pace in its actions and its speech. It tends to focus more on play and craft and does not rely on visual and auditory 'attention grabbers'. *Playschool* brings your child closer to

what is going on and has a much more personal feel to it.
Instructions are slow and clear and give your child time to act,
if he chooses, on what he has just heard.

In choosing programs, try to aim for effective viewing that
is only one part of daily family interaction, play and
education. The guidelines will help you achieve this.
Remember that you can restrict and negotiate which
programs are seen, even with a three-year-old. This will
encourage him to plan, to be selective and to savour his
program rather than just watching an endless stream.

CHAPTER FOUR

LEARNING TO TALK IN SPECIAL SITUATIONS

Language development in more challenging environments

Parlez-vous English?
Growing up bilingual

Millions of children around the world are exposed to two or sometimes even more languages. This might be because the parents speak more than one language or because a child moves to live in another country. It can also be the result of the general increased interest in foreign languages, which has meant that many young children are placed in various forms of foreign language learning environments.

Research to date has not consistently shown bilingualism to have either positive or negative effects on the child's development. However, it is common for bilingualism to bring many advantages to a person, both as a youngster and later as an adult. Your child is very lucky if he can speak more than one language, because many extra opportunities will be open to him. He could more easily live and work in another country.

Another language will also open his mind to a wider variety of ideas, cultures and experiences. Imagine his delight at being able to read road signs in a foreign language, or his pleasure at being able to speak to Grandma in Italian, or read letters from her.

Sometimes a child learning two languages will mix them both within the same utterance before he is aware of having two languages in his environment. However, he gradually learns to separate them, and language mixing is unusual after four years of age.

Bilingual adults sometimes use 'code switching', a conscious or purposeful switching of the two languages within one sentence or between sentences. Code switching is skilful, showing that the speaker has a good grasp of both languages, but it can also be detrimental if used by parents in front of young children who are trying to learn the languages. Young children may become confused and be unsure of which words belong to which language.

Because bilingual children may receive less exposure to each language, it may take them more time to achieve a similar language level to monolingual children. However, nearly all studies suggest that the bilingual child eventually 'catches up' after increased exposure.

Features of bilingual development

- There is usually an initial stage in which a child mixes languages.

- There can be a slow separation of the two languages.

- One language system can influence the other.

- One of the two languages usually becomes dominant.

- There can be a rapid shift in use when the language in the environment changes. Even if the second language hasn't been spoken for some time, a bilingual speaker is able to just 'slot in' to the new environment.

Source: Arnberg (1987) and other studies.

How can you help your child?

The main processes involved in language learning are the same whether your child is learning one or more than one language. But do you teach both languages simultaneously or successively one after the other? Both ways can result in the child being successful with both languages.

Parents might choose any of the following strategies to raise a child bilingually.

- An initial one-language strategy — your child learns one language first before another one is introduced.
- One person/one language method — Mum may decide to speak her native language whilst Dad uses English.
- A mixed language strategy — this is where any language may be used at any time.
- Speaking only the minority language in your home whilst your child is exposed to the other language at pre-school and other settings.

You can also make a choice about the degree of bilingualism exposure and use. As with all language learning, it should be fun! Use singing books and role-playing activities to teach the minority language in your home. Other ideas include borrowing library books and subscribing to children's magazines in the minority language. Many storybook cassettes are available, and video and television programs are also a great source of information and stimulation for learning.

Encourage your child's playgroup or kindergarten staff to become more interested in multiculturalism and the fostering of bilingualism. At the kindergarten you can display signs and labelled posters in various languages. You and other bilingual parents could go to the kindergarten and have fun teaching sessions with all the children. The children will love learning to count in four different languages or to sing a nursery rhyme in German.

Bilingual children with speech and language problems

What happens if you are a bilingual family and your child has a speech or language problem? Every situation is different and it really depends on the nature and severity of the problem. If a problem arises, we would encourage you to discuss it with a speech pathologist.

In cases where the child may just have some immaturities in sound development, there is no need to stop using either language. In some cases it may be advisable to encourage only the use of the majority language for a period of time until the child catches up.

There have been situations when a child has severe language problems and therefore needs to concentrate on just one language until his skills improve. This might mean discontinuing attendance at a non-English language school, for example, until English skills improve. If the problem is severe, chances are it is obvious in both languages.

Grandparents and other extended family members often become concerned when the child has to concentrate on one language. They feel the child will never learn enough of the native language to talk effectively with them. They need to be reassured that the child will learn the native language but maybe just not as early as they had hoped. Once the problem is sorted out in English, the child can then learn the other language. Often, all that is required is for the parents (who spend so much one-to-one time with the young child) to use English, although it is inevitable that they will be exposed to the other language at family gatherings.

If the child with a problem is in the care of a non-English speaker or a very poor English speaker a large part of the time, this needs to be discussed with your child's speech pathologist. If you, as a bilingual family, are at any time concerned about your child's speech and language we recommend you seek advice.

Extended family members often comfort the parents by telling them that it is 'just the two languages that are making the child slower to talk'. Sometimes this may be the case but often a speech problem has nothing to do with the bilingual background. It is more reassuring to seek help rather than let the child's problem become worse so that you have regrets later on.

In spite of the risk of delay in development a very large percentage of young children can learn more than one language without any problems and as a result reap the social and cultural gains that bilingualism has to offer.

The more the merrier
Multiple birth children

If you have twins, you will already be aware of the day-to-day joys and hassles. You might have two for the price of one, but you also have twice the work and twice the exhaustion — hopefully it leads to twice the fun.

One in 90 births is twins and one in 200 is triplets. These odds are increased with a strong family history or participation in artificial fertility programs. In this section we have used the term 'twins' as these are the most common multiple births, but of course the same advice applies to larger multiples!

There is a general belief that multiple birth children are more likely to have delayed speech and language than single births. Many do and many do not. Discussions about language development in twins may be likened to discussions about language development in children of bilingual backgrounds. Children from both groups are at risk of language delay but if they receive adequate and correct input from birth, the risk of a delay is minimised.

Parents of twins sometimes say: 'They sit and chatter and amuse each other all day'. This may mean they are less demanding but it may also mean their language development is suffering as a result. Children need a model to copy when learning a new skill. If young twins spend much of their time alone together, they have only each other to copy. They are less exposed to the adult model. Each is also much less exposed to the adult model *alone*, and this is the critical factor. Each infant needs regular one-to-one time with the parent if language skills are to develop adequately.

It is not unusual for a twin who is more noisy, outgoing and demanding to get more attention than the quieter one. However, we must be careful of classifying them as 'the dominant one' and 'the quiet one'. This creates stereotypes and leads us to have different expectations for each child. We will, in turn, always expect the more dominant child to say more and the quieter child to say less.

> *Children need a model to copy when learning a new skill.*
>
> *Each infant needs regular one-to-one time with the parent if language skills are to develop adequately.*

Furthermore, because twins usually relate to each other so well, they are not expected to relate to others as well as a single child might. The pressure is therefore not as great to make themselves understood and express their thoughts clearly. For this reason, too, parents should try to have *one-to-one* time with each child. If this is not possible to organise, try to address each child individually by always directing questions and comments to each one rather than to both at once. Try not to anticipate their needs, either jointly or individually, but always give them the chance to express their own needs. Remember that you are doing this not only for the sake of their language development but also for the sake of their social development. Sending one twin to a friend's place to play gives each the opportunity to interact alone and not rely on the other. It also gives the parent more one-to-one time with the child who stays home.

We all know of some sets of twins who have been delayed in their language development and unfortunately this has been accepted as a 'normal part of being a twin'. This need not be the case. It is important to remember that twins and other multiple birth children have the same potential for good speech and language as other children and we must not expect otherwise just because there is more than one.

Research has shown that, on average, at the time they start school twins (especially boys) are six to nine months behind single-born children in their overall language skills. A delay in language development can result in a delay in imaginative play and also in social behaviour towards peers and teachers. Twins are the same as single children, in that early speech and language problems can lead to later problems with reading, writing and spelling. Therefore early and appropriate language input is important. If you are concerned at any time, contact a speech pathologist.

~

CHAPTER FIVE

TALKING ABOUT BEHAVIOUR

Using speech to encourage positive behaviour

We don't wish to become bogged down with the subject of discipline. Discipline is an issue for all parents at some stage and there are many books already which cover this topic thoroughly.

However, your child's behaviours, both positive and negative, are forms of communication. Hence you can use your own communication skills and your knowledge of your child's language ability to encourage positive behaviour, to avoid potentially difficult situations and to manage your child when he is naughty.

As with other aspects of development, the teaching and learning of appropriate behaviour begins at birth. At first,

No!

No!

No!

This is also the time when your child greatly increases his use of the word 'no'. After all, he has heard it so many times!

How many different ways can you ask your child to stop an activity without using 'no'?

babies need to feel secure and require lots of reassurance. But you need to find a healthy balance: you don't want to control your child so much that he becomes too frightened to try new activities and experiment with new ideas.

When my son was just beginning to enjoy splashing in the water he had grommets (tubes) inserted in his ears. I was so anxious about him getting an infection that I would panic, shout or grab him (sometimes all three at once!) every time water crept up near his ears. I was so successful at encouraging fear of water that it took six years and a lot of hard work for him to overcome this fear.

It is very important that you give your child as much (or more) attention when he is happy and playing well as when he is crying or naughty. Your child needs to know which behaviour is the appropriate one — how is he supposed to know unless you tell him?

Try to find something to praise about your child's behaviours every hour of the day. Some days you might feel you have to look hard to find it, but you will. Try:

'Good girl, did you do that all by yourself? Clever girl!'
or
'That's nice playing, you two. You are sharing nicely together.'

Remember that it takes them time to learn, and children need reminders over and over again, given in a positive way.

Toddlers are inquisitive and often not in control of their behaviour. They have to learn to take turns and share, or to wait. Toddlers love to copy you, so watch your own behaviour. It's not fair to have one rule for the children and another for the grown-ups.

This is also the time when your child greatly increases his use of the word 'no'. After all, he has heard it so many times! It might be possible to prevent such a negative response by limiting your own use of the word. How many different ways can you ask your child to stop an activity without using 'no'?

When your child becomes mobile and starts talking, you may find your expectations increase enormously. If we demand too much of our children we may find an increase in temper tantrums are the result. We all get frustrated if we find a task too hard or are expected to 'perform' in a different situation. These feelings are increased when a well-meaning friend lets us know that we are failing.

Your toddler will only grasp the basics of an activity. He may in fact be trying to be helpful when he throws his china plate onto the floor — didn't he see you throw his plastic cup into the kitchen sink only this morning? Someone needs to explain the difference between china and plastic and between the sink and the floor!

Your child eventually has to learn that there are different ways of doing something. You may turn a blind eye to drinking his soup straight from the bowl at home, but it is not acceptable when you are out in company.

If we use our language wisely we can try to phrase our requests positively rather than concentrate on the negative behaviour. We want to teach our children the appropriate behaviour, so just complaining about his irritating behaviour doesn't tell him what he should be doing.

INSTEAD OF:	HOW ABOUT TRYING:
Oh, do stop whining.	I'll listen when you use a normal voice.
Don't slam the door when you go out!	Can you shut the door gently, please? Thank you.
Stop shouting!	Use a quiet voice, please.

If you want to try to change your child's behaviour make sure you give a clear message. Let him know what you want him to *do* and possibly why. A calm firm voice is more effective with a young child than shouting. A screaming voice conveys the message that you are angry. You may find that your child is so upset by the atmosphere shouting creates that he doesn't even listen to the message.

Yes!

Yes!

Yes!

Good Girl...

Good Boy...

Try to find something to praise about your child's behaviours every hour of the day.

INSTEAD OF:	HOW ABOUT TRYING:
Isn't there something you're supposed to do?	Please turn off the TV. Thank you.
Why is the Lego all over the floor?	Put your Lego back in the box, please.
Stop interrupting. It's very irritating.	Please wait until I've finished.
Stop doing that, you dirty boy.	Stop spitting right now.
Stop! That's not where the cornflakes go.	Put the cornflakes in the bowl.

Try avoiding commands or questions that can be answered with 'no'.

Most parents eventually want their children to become independent: to make choices for themselves and to reason why they make a certain choice. Being able to choose helps your child realise that what he thinks *is* important and that he *can* influence an event or activity. Children need practice at this. Wherever possible give simple choices:

'Let's go to the shop. Shall we walk or go by car?'

If you do give a choice, you need to respect the response. If he chooses to go by car only to have you overriding his decision by saying

'No, it's such a nice day I think we will walk',

where was the choice for your child?

Following on from this, make sure you're not giving a choice when in fact there isn't one. It's inviting a tantrum to ask your child what he would like for lunch when you only have peanut butter. Similarly, a question such as

'Are you going to come and have your bath now?'

'I can do this myself.'

Becoming independent, being able to choose helps your child realise that what he thinks is important and that he can influence an event or activity.

is unnecessary if in fact there is no choice. A positively phrased statement is more appropriate:

'It's bath time now.'

Treat your child with the respect you give to any adult. If you can tell your child what to do and expect an immediate response, then perhaps it should work both ways. If you can demand

'Come on! We're late. Get into the car now!',

then perhaps your child has the right to demand

'Get me a drink now!'

Using 'please' and 'thank you' will teach him a polite approach.

Giving advance warning of a change of activity can prevent tantrums as well as communicating your intentions to your child. Imagine watching your favourite TV program and your partner walks in and demands

'Turn the TV off. I want to go out for a drink!'

Impressed? Your child is a person with feelings, too, not an object to be ordered about.

A warning will also prepare your child to adjust to a change in circumstances.

'Three more throws and I have to get dinner ready.'

'When the advertisements come on, we have to go to the shops. We need some food to eat.'

Try to help your child to understand and take the consequences of his actions. If your child makes such a fuss that you decide to let him wear his socks and sandals on a rainy day, then he has to put up with wet feet and not expect a change of footwear to magically appear when he feels uncomfortable.

Constant threats are not helpful. Constant warnings might scare your child: 'Be careful, you'll fall', and 'I told you so' when he does fall contributes nothing but bad feeling to the situation.

Consistent handling is extremely important. Not only should one person be consistent but parents need to agree on management or the child will learn how to manipulate the situation and play one partner off against the other.

Be sure of your facts before making a stand — the offence may not be as serious as it first seems and once you have made a decision on how to handle the situation, you will have to stick with it. If you keep changing your mind or 'giving in', your child will learn that it's well worth his nagging and keeping up the pressure. By doing it, he usually gets what he wants.

Consistency will help your child learn the rules and know where his boundaries are. When you say 'no' make sure you mean 'no' and not 'maybe' or 'I'm open to persuasion'.

Feelings and self-esteem

Your child has feelings and you can help him to recognise and understand them, as well as the feelings of others.

Even when he is very young, give a name to his mood. If someone takes his toy, acknowledge that he is angry. Let him know that you understand:

'You are angry because that boy took your ball away.'

If there is a dispute with another child, encourage him to express his feelings and explain what has upset him:

'That hurt when you pinched me.'

Make sure that your own feelings are clarified. If you are upset, let your child know that it is not because he is being very naughty:

'Sorry I shouted, mummy is so tired today.'

Your child needs to know that whatever your mood or whatever the behaviour, you still love him. He will be secure knowing this. Never threaten to withdraw affection. This is both cruel and dangerous. When your child has behaved badly, make it very clear that it is the behaviour which is the problem not the child. The slight shift of emphasis is important for your child's self-esteem.

Encourage your child to feel pleased with his *own* behaviour and successes. He doesn't need to be completely dependent on other people for praise:

'You read that all by yourself. You must be so proud of yourself.'

Your message can help develop your child's positive self-esteem.

Handling difficult behaviours

When our children are doing things we think are naughty, most of us do not stop to think — we just react. It might be easier said than done, but try to stop and think before you respond. What is your child trying to communicate to you? Why is he doing it?

Ask yourself some of the following questions, and remember that a child's age and developmental level may make your responses different for different children.

Is it Really Naughty?

How serious is the naughty behaviour? Is it physically dangerous? Did it hurt someone?

Do you think your child understands that the behaviour is naughty? Or is it time to start teaching some simple rules like: 'No hitting, it hurts.'

Throughout this book we have referred to expectations. Consider whether you have appropriate expectations for your child. Is it possible that they are too high? Are you expecting your two-year-old to behave like your neighbour's four-year-old?

Before you respond to your child's behaviour, remember that you are wanting to communicate a message to your child. Your response needs to be appropriate for the behaviour. If you are shouting and screaming all the time, then your child may find it so predictable that he starts to ignore your voice — your shouting may become yet another background noise and lose its effect. In a dangerous situation, your child's immediate response may save a life. Say, for instance, his ball runs onto the road and he tries to run after it. You will shout at him to stop. Hopefully your child will realise from your voice that this is important and stop.

Perhaps for a more routine situation like books all over the floor, a positive comment along the lines already discussed would be more appropriate:

'Can you help me put all these books back on the shelf?'

Stop and Think

Is it really naughty?

Am I over-reacting?

Why is my child doing this?

What will help my child not to do it again?

INSTEAD OF:	HOW ABOUT TRYING:
You are naughty to throw toys about the room.	Throwing toys is naughty. Something might get broken.
You are so naughty. Why do you kick other children?	Kicking hurts. You are not to do it.

TACTICS

Ignore

Distract

Prevent

Give
Reasons

*The best strategy
for dealing with
poor behaviour is
to encourage and
teach positive
alternative
behaviour.*

AM I OVER-REACTING?

If you are, then why? Are you tired or unwell? If you are, don't set yourself and your family numerous or unrealistic goals for the day. Take it easy — go to the park, get a take-away dinner.

WHY IS MY CHILD DOING THIS?

Is he bored and seeking attention? Have you had a busy day? Is your child letting you know that he would like some of your time?

Is he frustrated? Is the activity too difficult or does he need some help? You may be able to ease the frustration by breaking down the activity into smaller steps. Sometimes frustration may arise because in fact the task is too easy. Just because he enjoyed doing the activity once, doesn't mean he wants to keep doing it.

What will help my child learn not to do it again?

When you do discipline your child, you want him to learn how to manage himself more effectively and cope with the world. Listed below are some general tactics. If you would like to investigate this further, there is some suggested reading at the end of this book.

IGNORING THE INCIDENT

This can be easier said than done. Any parent who has a whining child around will know how difficult this is, but it can be effective. Ignoring only works if your child is seeking your attention and the behaviour, such as using naughty words, can be ignored. Not commenting can often defuse the situation. Toddler tantrums may occur less frequently if they are ignored.

DISTRACTING HIM

The success of this method depends on your child's age. Older children are more difficult to distract, but it's relatively easy in the baby/toddler group. Try to be realistic. Expecting your toddler to share can be unrealistic, but finding another toy of interest — especially if it's similar — can be helpful. Sometimes you may be able to distract both children from the offending objects. Perhaps you can suddenly see a cat in the garden.

PREVENTION

When your child becomes mobile you'll find that he gets into everything. You can remove your child from the cause of trouble, but it's often more appropriate to rearrange the environment to avoid trouble occurring in the first place. It may be impossible for your newly-standing child to ignore the temptation of a dangling tablecloth.

GIVING SIMPLE REASONS

Offering a simple reason or setting the rules ('Hitting hurts, no hitting.') may be far more effective than shouting. For very young children, using an exaggerated expression in your voice will help:

'Oh! Hot! Hurts!'

TIME OUT

Your child can be put into 'time out' by removing him and placing him in a situation (such as his bedroom or a corner of the room) where he is given no attention at all. Or you might leave the room yourself.

Time out gives you and your child a chance to calm down and save face. You'll need to explain it in advance — don't just spring it on him. And make sure he knows when time out finishes — when a clock rings, for example.

For a small child, it's best to keep it very brief. It is best to use time out only for behaviours that you just cannot ignore.

PUNISHMENT

Punishment in the form of hitting is not recommended at all. It communicates the message that it's all right to be aggressive and hit someone if you don't like what they are doing. Remember that punishment is not discipline but a sign that discipline has been unsuccessful. When it is really necessary, punishment should never be humiliating and once administered the incident should be forgotten.

The best strategy for dealing with poor behaviour is to encourage and teach positive alternative behaviour.

~

CHAPTER SIX

COMMON QUESTIONS ABOUT TALKING

Can ear, nose and throat problems affect speech development?

Ear, nose and throat (or ENT) problems are very common in childhood and may account for repeated minor illness as well as frequent visits to doctors and even admissions to hospital.

Repeated attacks of hay fever, obstructed breathing, sinusitis, tonsillitis and middle ear infections can contribute to poor general development and reduced mental alertness. Children with recurrent episodes of tonsillitis, ear infections or sinusitis often show a lack of appetite and therefore sometimes have a slower rate of physical growth. They may seem to be always tired and listless and this must affect their rate of learning.

A child who is ill may not feel well enough to do much talking, or well-meaning adults may encourage a more passive behaviour which allows the child's needs to be met without having to talk. For instance, every time the child cries he may be given a drink immediately without having to ask for it.

Sucking is a basic physiological function.

Sucking is fun and makes a baby feel good.

Be careful not to use a dummy as a plug to keep the baby's mouth closed and hence keep him quiet.

Many children suffer from upper respiratory infection and do not complain about the pain. This may go unnoticed during the early preschool years and, as a result the child's hearing may have been fluctuating all that time. If this happens often enough at a critical time in development, speech and language can be delayed. Therefore, the importance of attending the baby health clinic for regular checks — which include hearing tests — cannot be stressed enough.

Babies start to hear during the last months of pregnancy and are born with full hearing. A baby of six months will turn its head to locate a sound. The onset of the first words at around 12 months may indicate to the parents that hearing is adequate for speech and language development. However, this situation may change as a result of ear infections or other illness. Therefore, if at any time you have doubts about your infant's hearing, take him to your baby clinic or to your doctor. A screening test will show whether further testing is required.

It is important to be aware of the difference between hearing and listening. Some preschoolers are simply stubborn and may refuse to listen. If you examine a variety of situations you will notice that your child may not respond to you when you ask him to pick up his toys but he will respond if he hears you rattle the biscuit barrel. Such a child does not have a hearing problem — he is just being a 'selective listener'!

What is the effect of sucking dummies, thumbs and bottles?

Sucking is a basic physiological function which has a role to play in developing breathing coordination and speech. It helps develop a sense of touch and sight and helps in the development of the teeth, jaw and facial muscles. Most babies are soothed by sucking whether it's on the breast, bottle, hand or dummy.

Sucking is fun and makes a baby feel good. Although there is an anti-dummy movement, if presented with the choice of an irritable baby or using a dummy, perhaps like us you'll choose the latter!

However, be careful not to use a dummy as a plug to keep the baby's mouth closed and hence keep him quiet. Constant use can lead to passive children who are only happy when

'Silly
Mummy
lost the
dummies.'

If you are

concerned and

want your infant

to stop using it,

then try not

replacing the

dummy next time

it is lost! Try

explaining that you

have lost the

dummy and look

everywhere for it

with your child.

Make sure they

have all been

thrown away so

there is no chance

of finding one.

they have something in their mouths. It may also produce children who have no desire to talk. It's easier to say nothing and just point to a cup than to take the dummy out and say 'Drink please'.

If a child tries to talk with the dummy in his mouth, remind him that you would like to be able to understand him and that it's easier to talk without a dummy.

A dummy should not be used to distract a child who is seeking adult attention and involvement in an activity. It is not a substitute for parent-child interaction.

Thumb-sucking is also worth mentioning at this point and much of what is said about the dummy can apply to thumb-sucking as well. Prolonged thumb-sucking can interfere with the development of your child's teeth. It may also cause the child's tongue to rest in a more forward position in the mouth which can lead to abnormal swallowing patterns, tongue thrusting and poor production of some speech sounds, as in a lisp.

You might wonder if there is ever a 'right' time to take the dummy away from the child. It is a good idea to be guided by your child to some extent — when you sense he is only using it out of habit take it away and see what happens. If a baby starts to spit the dummy out or push the tongue forward when sucking on it, the use of it should be questioned.

If you are concerned and want your infant to stop using it, then try not replacing the dummy next time it is lost! However, we all know that's not as easy as it sounds. Rather than making it a battleground, try explaining that you have lost the dummy and look everywhere for it with your child helping. Make sure they have all been thrown away so there is no chance of finding one. Use your child's language ability. 'Silly mummy lost the dummies. What would you like to take to bed? Teddy?' At the outside, try to 'lose' the dummy by the time your child is two. You might then suggest, when the last one is 'lost', that shops don't sell dummies for big children of two or more.

Like the dummy, thumb sucking can often be stopped by reminding the child of his level of maturity. This works particularly well if there is a younger baby in the household and the elder child can see that only babies and not 'big children' suck their thumbs or use a dummy.

Or try talking about a 'naughty thumb' (rather than a 'naughty child'). 'Can you be the boss and teach the thumb not to go in your mouth?' is an approach worth trying. The older child might like to bandage the 'naughty thumb', so that he is reminded by the feel of the bandages to take the thumb away. Praise him for being a good teacher when you see him without the thumb in his mouth.

There are many different techniques to try (such as nail paint), but working positively with your child should be much more successful than making him feel inferior.

Bottle feeding is meant to be like breast feeding in that the infant gets regular good sucking practice. The type of teat is therefore important and should not allow the infant to just gulp to get his milk. Hard teats tend to pull a baby's jaw in narrower and this forces him to open his lips and breathe through his mouth. This may result in the top teeth being pushed forward or the development of a tongue thrusting pattern. As stated earlier, both of these can cause problems with speech sound development. Because of this, it is advisable to make the transition to cup drinking by the age of 12 months.

Recent research has shown a renewed increase of teeth cavities in toddlers as a result of them being given drinks containing sugar in their bottle. Many parents use the bottle as an easy way to calm their child, distract him, get him off to sleep or simply to keep the child busy. As with the dummy, the child just learns to satisfy his other needs by drinking.

Like the dummy, thumb sucking can often be stopped by reminding the child of his level of maturity. This works particularly well if there is a younger baby in the household.

'Can you be the boss and teach the thumb not to go in your mouth?'

The speech pathologist says my child has a tongue thrust. What does this mean? Why is the dentist concerned?

Tongue thrusting is a way of swallowing. In normal swallowing, the back teeth are in alignment while the tongue pushes up and then pulls back. In tongue thrusting, the tongue pushes forward against the upper front teeth or protrudes between the teeth.

All babies use a thrusting swallow at first, but should change over during the preschool years. Some, however, don't make the change, for a number of possible reasons including:

• thumb or dummy-sucking;
• enlarged tonsils or adenoids;

- allergies and nasal congestion;
- very high, narrow palate;
- poor muscle coordination.

Tongue thrusting is frequently associated with a lisp. The dentist will be concerned because the constant pressure of the tongue against the teeth can contribute to dental problems or malformation, requiring orthodontic treatment.

A speech pathologist can help your child to retrain his tongue posture.

When is dribbling a problem?

Dribbling is a normal part of development, especially from four to six months. This is usually at the time when the baby is ready for eating solids. Copious dribbling can also be a sign of teething, thrush or a mouth infection.

Dribbling can occur as a child is learning a new motor skill and later, in the 15 to 24 month period, they may dribble when concentrating in play or when drawing.

Some children do continue to have problems with dribbling in association with other oral problems. Obviously good control of the tongue, lips and jaw are necessary for speech development. Some children present as being sensitive around the mouth area and lack awareness of oral muscles. They may dribble, mouth breathe, dislike being touched around the mouth, not eat solid foods and be generally fussy eaters.

To help infants gain greater control of their tongue and lips, you can play games involving the mouth from a young age. Blow raspberries, blow bubbles, blow out candles and blow and drink through straws. All of these activities will make the child more aware of his mouth and strengthen the muscles. If you are concerned, consult a speech pathologist for advice.

What if my child has to go to hospital?

For some children a hospital stay may prove to be an important stage in social and emotional development and play a part in the 'growing up' process. On the other hand, a stay in hospital can be most traumatic for a toddler and he needs to be prepared well before admission. There are many factors to consider — pain and unpleasantness, parent separation, loneliness, boredom, fear, unfamiliarity and parent anxieties.

Some of the warning signs that the stay in hospital has been traumatic may include a regression to more immature behaviours such as thumb sucking, wanting a dummy and even bed-wetting for the older child. An extended stay may limit the child's contact with peers and may provide little stimulation and opportunity for the child to speak. It is possible that if hospitalisation occurs at a critical time in the child's language development it may cause a delay; for example, a child may have just started talking at about 14 months and be using several single words when he goes into hospital — he may then stop talking and present six months later with no improvement.

Similar effects on language development may result from other traumatic incidents such as the child's

mother or father going away for a few weeks or a new baby coming into the family.

Could my child be tongue-tied?

A tongue tie is where the skin connecting the tongue tip to the bottom of the mouth is very short. This may limit tongue movements. In very severe cases, the production of some speech sounds may be distorted and affect the development of teeth.

However, in our experience it is rarely necessary to surgically clip the tongue, as children learn to compensate. Surgery does not necessarily alter speech clarity.

Are my child's mouth muscles working properly?

Some children do have poor oral coordination and weak muscle control. Look for a child who:

- constantly has his mouth open;
- is constantly dribbling (not only when teething);
- has food falling out of his mouth when eating; or
- is a slow eater, has trouble chewing or regurgitates food down his nose.

All of these signs can be associated with speech problems. For example, when a word combines sounds produced at the back and the front of the mouth ('kettle'), one or both of the sounds may be omitted or they may occur in the wrong place. Similarly, words with several syllables may be shortened or mumbled.

Speech pathologists can suggest exercise programs to improve the accuracy and speed of oral muscles.

When is a lisp a problem?

There are two types of lisps. The one we are all most familiar with is the one demonstrated by cute little three-year-olds whose tongues poke out between their teeth when they say 's' or 'z'. This lisp should be outgrown by the time your child is five. After five, or if at any time the bite of your child's teeth is affected, then further advice should be sought from a speech pathologist and orthodontist.

The other type of lisp is where the tongue usually cannot be seen but the 's' sound is slushy. If your child has this type of lisp you should see a speech pathologist, because he will not grow out of this abnormal pattern.

Does my child have hearing problems?

Normal hearing is a prerequisite for speech development. Early childhood check-ups will screen your child's hearing and we recommend that you attend annually until he starts school. While most of the speech difficulties we see are not caused by hearing problems, early detection means early prevention and treatment.

Signs of hearing problems include:

- not paying attention when being spoken to;
- constantly asking for what is said to be repeated;
- mispronouncing words slightly by confusing sounds;
- behavioural problems;
- frequent upper respiratory infections;
- not using speech very much;
- staring at people's mouths when they talk.

Is my child a stutterer?

It can be quite a shock for parents when their child wakes one morning and gets stuck on his words: 'I-I-I-I want a drink.' A stutter can appear between the ages of two and seven. A family history of stuttering increases the risk. Numerous repetitions, prolongation of words ('Mmmmummy') and funny faces are also signs of a stutter. If this occurs and you or your child are feeling frustrated, you should seek advice as soon as possible, preferably during the preschool years. Therapy in preschool children can be very effective.

Don't feel anxious about commenting to your child about his stuttering, but do it gently. 'Gut feeling' advice is often appropriate:

'Slow down a bit. Take your time'.

I-I-I-I
want...

A stutter can appear between the ages of two and seven. A family history of stuttering increases the risk.

Seek advice as soon as possible and preferably during the preschool years. Therapy in preschool children can be very effective.

By the time your child starts school, he should be talking almost as well as you do. Most speech and language problems can be detected before a child starts school.

With a child of three or more, you can be more direct:

'You said "Mum" lots of times then. See if you can say it just once. "Mum, can I have a drink please."'

Use slower, steady speech to model for your child.

This is contrary to the more traditional advice to ignore the stutter and just wait patiently for your child to finish — current research shows beyond question that your child will benefit from your comments. (The approach to an adult with a stutter is very different.)

Children can go through a period of 'normal non-fluency', especially when their speech takes off and they have a lot to say. They talk like an adult but are not quite ready to do so, resulting in the repetition of a few words. If non-fluency continues for more than three months, you should consult a speech pathologist.

What should I do if my child can't say sounds properly? Is he just lazy?

It is unlikely that speech problems are the result of laziness. If your child has trouble with sounds, try some of the activities suggested on pages 40–42. However, if the problems persist, do seek advice from a speech pathologist.

Shall I wait until my child starts school before doing anything about his speech or language?

No! By the time your child starts school, he should be talking almost as well as you do. Most speech and language problems can be detected before a child starts school.

Whatever the age of your child, if you are anxious it is better to be safe than sorry and have your child checked out. Waiting too long may make his problem worse.

Is my child 'backwards' or retarded because he has speech problems?

Children who are intellectually disabled frequently have unclear speech. However, if your child has a specific speech and/or language problem it does *not* mean he is intellectually retarded. Even gifted and talented children have speech difficulties.

A speech pathologist will assess all aspects of your child's development and discuss it all with you.

It is true to say that the earlier your child can develop his communication skills the more he reduces the chances of having difficulties with reading and writing.

What possible reason could there be for my child's speech problem?

Finding the exact cause of a problem can be difficult. Some speech problems and learning difficulties can be inherited, just like any other characteristic. However, the following are the most common reasons:

- Hearing loss — even a temporary loss creates a delay in speech development.
- Language delay — perhaps the child is just immature in the area of language but is progressing through the appropriate stages.
- Language disorder — sometimes a child with normal intellectual ability can have difficulty understanding what is said to him or expressing himself.
- Oral deformity — such as cleft palate.
- Poor oral coordination — some children have difficulty learning how to coordinate their mouth movements to produce speech.

Unfortunately we often simply don't know why some children have difficulties and others don't. Some children will make rapid progress on a home-based program while others require intensive professional input over many months. The earlier they start, the better the outcome.

Will computers help my child's language?

Many of us shy away from computers because of their seeming complexity, but many of our children are being exposed to computers at a very young age.

Speech pathologists in private practice may be listed in the Yellow Pages, or your family doctor or child health worker should be able to recommend one. Speech pathologists also work in community health centres, Education Departments, Children's Services Offices and kindergartens.

Computers can assist the young child to develop skills in several areas — including looking, listening, hand and finger control, turn taking and language learning — but they should be regarded as complementary to your child's traditional learning experiences and never as a substitute.

Computer software can provide opportunities for your child to develop his imagination and problem-solving abilities. It can also help in the development of rhythm. Appropriate software can also enhance the understanding of many language concepts, such as colours, numbers, opposites and letters.

Remember that your child interacts with the software rather than the computer, so it is important to supply a good range. As with toys, it's a good idea to provide a mix of software that is educational and software which is just for fun. There is an enormous range of software now available — make time to go and talk to a local retailer.

While some children talk very little while alone at a computer, others give a running commentary on every move, 'thinking aloud', giggling and exclaiming. If more than one person is involved, then turn taking is practised and a lot of talking can take place.

If you have a printer attached to your computer, your four-year-old can experiment with printing out words or even writing letters. These letters can then be illustrated or even made into birthday cards.

Concern has been expressed in recent years that children may be stunting their language development by using computers. We believe that, like many things, they should be used in moderation. We worry if a child is spending hours at the keyboard on a sunny day.

Is using a computer better than watching television? As we have said earlier, television is useful if it is the basis of an active exchange between you and your child. While television and computer screens look the same, there is an important difference in that watching a television screen is passive, while using a computer screen is very active: the child manipulates what is on the screen, pushes the keys, takes turns if with another person and probably talks more than when watching television.

How will I recognise if my child has a speech or language problem?

You would be best to seek advice from a speech pathologist if your child:

- is not using some single words by eighteen months;
- is not putting words together by two years;
- is not using three- to four-word sentences by three to three and a half years;
- is using immature sentences;
- is hard to understand by age three;
- is making sound errors well beyond the appropriate age;
- is not responding to sounds;
- does not seem to listen and understand instructions;
- is using a nasal, loud jerky or hoarse voice; or
- is so hesitant or repetitive when talking that it makes the listener anxious.

What do I need to do to see a speech pathologist?

Usually you can just telephone and give your child's details over the phone. Sometimes you will need a doctor's referral so check what the procedure is. Many speech pathologists (especially in hospitals) have waiting lists, so put your child's name down as soon as possible. An appointment can always be cancelled if it is not needed when the time comes.

Speech pathologists in private practice may be listed in the Yellow Pages, or your family doctor or child health worker should be able to recommend one. Speech pathologists also work in community health centres, Education Departments, Children's Services Offices and kindergartens.

Developmental Checklist

The age groupings are only rough guidelines, so your child may not have all the skills listed. But if most of your child's skills fall one or more groups behind his age group's, we suggest you contact a speech pathologist.

0–3 MONTHS

By the time your child is 3 months, he can

UNDERSTANDING

- respond to sound — loud noise may still cause distress
- recognise familiar voices
- gaze at a speaker's face
- look at a clear, simple picture
- recognise familiar routines e.g. feeding

MOTOR SKILLS

- suck and swallow
- sleep for a great deal of the time not being fed
- move less jerkily
- kick legs vigorously

COMMUNICATION

- cry when hungry
- gurgle and make vowel-like sounds
- smile

SOCIAL SKILLS

- be unpredictable
- enjoy being cuddled and spoken to
- lift head to look around
- feel, taste, smell and hear

4–6 MONTHS

By the time your child is 6 months, he can

UNDERSTANDING

- turn head to find the source of sound
- be startled by loud noises
- recognise own name
- recognise names of familiar people e.g. Mum, Dad
- recognise difference between angry and friendly voices

MOTOR SKILLS

- look at hands and feet
- support head and chest with arms when on stomach
- try to roll over
- sit with or without support
- hold something in either hand
- bounce when held in standing position
- explore objects with the mouth

COMMUNICATION

- make sounds in response to speech
- make a variety of speech sounds
- use different cries to mean different things
- laugh and chuckle in play
- scream with annoyance
- shake rattle deliberately to make sound

SOCIAL SKILLS

- enjoy looking in the mirror
- recognise familiar situations e.g. bath time
- enjoy playing peek-a-boo
- purposely drop object to have it returned to him
- be friendly with strangers

7–9 MONTHS

By the time your child is 9 months, he can

UNDERSTANDING

- understand the word 'no'
- recognise common objects by name
- enjoy noise-making toys
- look at pictures when named

MOTOR SKILLS

- pick up cup/finger food etc.
- feed self with finger foods
- pull to standing position
- be mobile
- pick up small objects and put them into his mouth
- pick up, push and shove large things

COMMUNICATION

- copy speech sounds
- use a greater variety of sounds
- make noise with things on purpose
- use simple gestures, e.g. wave bye bye, clap
- shout to attract attention

SOCIAL SKILLS

- play an increasing variety of games e.g. pat-a-cake
- show anxiety when a familiar person leaves the room

- distinguish strangers from familiar faces
- manipulate objects with interest, passing them from hand to hand
- look for a toy falling over the edge of pram or table
- watch movements of other people

10–12 Months

By the time your child is 12 months, he can

UNDERSTANDING

- respond well to his name
- respond to familiar sounds e.g. phone ringing
- follow simple commands

MOTOR SKILLS

- sit on a chair
- drop things into a small opening
- crawl, scoot, creep or walk from one place to another
- point with index finger at objects he wants or which interest him
- use both hands freely (but he may show a preference for one)

COMMUNICATION

- respond by nodding or shaking his head
- use an increasing amount of speech and may sound as if he is talking
- vary pitch and loudness of sounds
- name familiar objects/people
- indicate his basic wants e.g. biscuit, juice

SOCIAL SKILLS

- play simple make-believe games
- use gestures e.g. waving
- help with dressing
- repeat activities to reproduce effects e.g. throwing objects deliberately onto the floor
- like to be constantly within sight and hearing of adults
- look in the correct place for toys which have rolled out of sight

13–18 Months

By the time your child is 18 months, he can

UNDERSTANDING

- shake his head appropriately for simple yes/no questions
- move rhythmically to music
- enjoy simple rhymes and songs
- understand many words and simple directions
- show at least one body part

MOTOR SKILLS

- walk well
- start and stop safely
- pick up a toy from the floor without falling
- spontaneously scribble when given a crayon
- turn 2 or 3 pages at a time
- pick up small beads etc with delicate first finger and thumb movement
- push, pull or carry toy while walking
- use a spoon to scoop
- no longer takes toys to the mouth

COMMUNICATION

- jabber tunefully to himself
- use some words correctly
- attempt to sing
- demand desired objects by pointing and talking/grunting
- echo the prominent or last word said to him
- initiate simple activities e.g. sweeping the floor or reading

SOCIAL SKILLS

- explore the environment energetically
- remember where objects belong
- play alone contentedly but likes to be near an adult
- still be emotionally dependent on a familiar adult
- alternate between clinging and resistance
- enjoy doing the same things over and over again

2 Years

By the time your child is 2 years, he can

UNDERSTANDING

- point to 5 body parts
- listen to a short story
- match sounds to animals
- recognise pictures and name them

MOTOR SKILLS

- throw a ball
- string large beads
- run fast
- turn one page at a time
- try to jump
- chew food well
- try to balance on one foot
- turn door handles

COMMUNICATION

- use his own name
- say two-word sentences e.g. more milk
- use words that tell what people or things do
- use words that tell about people and things
- sing some words to songs
- use many but not all sounds accurately
- use 50 or more words
- talk continually whilst playing
- constantly ask for names of objects

SOCIAL SKILLS

- show emotions
- copy housework
- feel frustrated easily
- try to comfort others
- follow Mum or Dad around the house copying domestic activities
- constantly demand Mum or Dad's attention
- tantrum when frustrated
- have no idea of sharing
- play near other children but not with them

2½ YEARS

By the time your child is 2½ years, he can

UNDERSTANDING

- enjoy familiar stories
- select correct items from a choice of 5 upon request
- understand many complex sentences

MOTOR SKILLS

- jump with two feet together
- sit on a tricycle and propel himself with feet

on the ground
- build a tower of 7 blocks
- eat skilfully with a spoon and fork
- walk upstairs alone
- kick a large ball
- push and pull toys skilfully

COMMUNICATION

- say his full name
- talk intelligibly to himself at play concerning events happening here and now
- use 200 or more recognisable words
- continually ask questions 'what?' 'where?'
- use pronouns 'I', 'me', and 'we'
- have the beginnings of a crude grammar e.g. 'I goed'
- have stopped using jargon
- have speech that might be non-fluent (similar to stuttering) in his eagerness to talk

SOCIAL SKILLS

- often be very active and restless
- engage in prolonged domestic make-believe play e.g. putting dolls to bed
- watch other children at play and occasionally join in for a few minutes
- have very little idea about sharing toys or adults' attention

3 YEARS

By the time your child is 3 years, he can

UNDERSTANDING

- listen eagerly to new stories

- seem to understand most of what is said to him
- begin to identify objects by use e.g. 'What do we eat with?'
- choose between objects
- show an understanding of past and present
- know several nursery rhymes

MOTOR SKILLS

- climb nursery equipment with agility
- turn around obstacles and corners when running
- stand momentarily on one foot
- walk on tiptoe
- copy a circle
- start cutting with scissors

COMMUNICATION

- talk in short sentences
- use a large vocabulary
- ask many questions — 'what?', 'where?' and 'who?'
- use speech that still has many errors
- name one colour
- use speech that may often have repetitions of words, especially when excited or anxious
- use plurals e.g. dogs
- carry on a simple conversation
- be understood most of the time within the family

SOCIAL SKILLS

- have general behaviour that's more amenable
- enjoy dramatic make-believe play including pretend objects and people
- join in play with other children inside and outdoors

- understand sharing, although won't always do so
- show affection for younger siblings
- do easy picture matching

4 YEARS

By the time your child is 4 years, he can

UNDERSTANDING

- locate the source of sound
- know several colours
- put simple objects into groups e.g. foods
- understand some opposites
- understand past, present and future

MOTOR SKILLS

- climb ladders and trees
- be an expert rider of a tricycle
- do a five- to ten-piece puzzle
- screw a lid onto a jar
- do simple block building
- match a simple bead or block design
- draw a basic picture of a man
- hop on one foot
- dress and undress except for laces and back buttons

COMMUNICATION

- use speech that is completely intelligible, with few sound substitutions remaining
- give a connected account of recent events and experiences
- constantly ask questions — 'why?', 'how?'
- ask what words mean
- listen to and tell long stories, sometimes confusing fact and fantasy

SOCIAL SKILLS

- take part in a short group time
- talk to friends while playing
- have general behaviour that is self-willed
- be inclined to verbal impertinence but can be affectionate and compliant
- need other children to play with and is alternatively cooperative and aggressive with them and with adults
- understand turn-taking
- show concern for younger siblings and sympathy for playmates in distress

5 YEARS

By the time your child is 5 years, he can

UNDERSTANDING

- appreciate the meaning of clock time in relation to the daily program
- understand most of what is heard
- understand right and left
- appreciate humour

MOTOR SKILLS

- run lightly on toes
- skip on alternate feet
- write a few letters
- draw a recognisable man
- be skilful in climbing, sliding and swinging
- use a knife and fork

COMMUNICATION

- speak in complete sentences
- use speech that is fluent and grammatical
- have articulation that is correct except for residual confusions in s/f/th and r/l/w/y groups
- define noun by use
- ask the meaning of abstract words

SOCIAL SKILLS

- have general behaviour that is more sensible, controlled and responsibly independent
- play complicated floor games
- choose own friends
- be cooperative with companions and understand the need for rules and fair play
- be protective towards other children
- continue a game from one day to another

APPENDICES
Appendix I

Children's booklist

Here are some suggestions for books to help promote language development. You may find many of them at your local library. Remember, too, that books make excellent presents.

TITLE	AUTHOR	PUBLISHER
NURSERY RHYMES AND RHYTHMICAL BOOKS		
Rhymes Around the Day	Jan Ormerod	Picture Puffin
Finger Rhymes	Traditional	Ladybird
Action Rhymes	Traditional	Ladybird
Too Many Monkeys	ill. Kelly Oechsli	Golden Storytime Book
The Boy with a Drum	David L Harrison	Golden Books
Hand, Hand, Fingers, Thumb	Al Perkins	Random House
The New Baby Calf	Edith Newlin Chase	Ashton Scholastic
Down in the Meadow	ill. Ezra Jack Keats	Ashton Scholastic
Over in the Meadow	ill. Mary Maki Rae	Picture Puffin

TITLE	AUTHOR	PUBLISHER
PICTURE BOOKS		
First Picture Books 1 - 5		Ladybird
Talkabout Series		Ladybird
Hop, Skip and Jump Book	Jack Kent	Random House Picture Book
500 Words to Grow On	ill. Harry McNaught	Random House Picture Book
The House	Carol Watson & Colin King	Rigby/Usborne
The Town	Carol Watson & Colin King	Rigby/Usborne
The Shop	Carol Watson & Colin King	Rigby/Usborne
REPETITIVE STORIES		
Cat on the Mat	Brian Wildsmith	Oxford
My Cat Likes to Hide in Boxes	Eve Sutton	Picture Puffin
Are You There, Bear?	Ron Maris	Picture Puffin
Just Like Daddy	Frank Asch	Carousel
The Animals of Farmer Jones	Leah Gale	Golden Books
Who Sank the Boat?	Pamela Allen	Nelson
Bertie and the Bear	Pamela Allen	Nelson
Jump, Frog, Jump	Robert Kalan	Corgi
Better Move On, Frog	Ron Maris	Picture Lion

TITLE	AUTHOR	PUBLISHER
DAILY SEQUENCES		
Doing the Washing	Sarah Garland	Picture Puffin
Lucy and Tom's Day	Shirley Hughes	Carousel/Picture Puffin
Lucy and Tom go to School	Shirley Hughes	Carousel
Lucy and Tom at the Seaside	Shirley Hughes	Carousel
On Friday Something Funny Happened	John Prater	Picture Puffin
Teddy Bear Gardener	Phoebe & June Worthington	Picture Puffin
One Hundred & One Things to Do with a Baby	Jan Ormerod	Lothrop
SIMPLE STORIES		
Noisy Nora	Rosemary Wells	Picture Lion
The Very Hungry Caterpillar	Eric Carle	Picture Puffin
I'm going for a Walk	Shigeo Waganabe	Picture Puffin
Rose's Walk	Pat Hutchins	Picture Puffin
Mr Smudge's Thirsty Day	Jonathan Gunson	Reed Methuen
The Last Puppy	Frank Asch	Carousel
Big Dog, Little Dog	P D Eastman	Picture Lion

SIMPLE STORIES CONT

TITLE	AUTHOR	PUBLISHER
There's a Hippopotamus On Our Roof Eating Cake	Hazel Edwards	Hodder & Stoughton
My Hippopotamus Is On Our Caravan Roof Getting Sunburnt	Hazel Edwards	Hodder & Stoughton
The Sick Cow	H E Todd & Val Biro	Picture Puffin
Sam Who Never Forgets	Eve Rice	Picture Puffin
Benny Bakes a Cake	Eve Rice	Picture Puffin
Harry the Dirty Dog	Gene Zion	Picture Puffin
Mr Brown's Magnificent Apple Tree	Yvonne Winer	Ashton Scholastic
The Tiger Who Came to Tea	Judith Kerr	Picture Lion
Happy Birthday, Sam	Pat Hutchins	Picture Puffin
Mr Gumpy's Outing	John Burningham	Picture Puffin
Geraldine's Blanket	Holly Keller	Picture Puffin
Sally's Secret	Shirley Hughes	Picture Lion
Well-loved Tales, The Gingerbread Boy, The Little Red Hen		Ladybird (Series 606D)

TITLE	AUTHOR	PUBLISHER

LONGER, MORE COMPLEX STORIES

Dogger	Shirley Hughes	Picture Lion
Alfie Gets in First	Shirley Hughes	Picture Lion
Alfie's Feet	Shirley Hughes	Picture Lion
Alfie Gives a Hand	Shirley Hughes	Picture Lion
An Evening at Alfie's	Shirley Hughes	Picture Lion
Big Joe's Trailer Truck	Joe Mathieu	Random House
Buttons	Tom Robinson	Picture Puffin
The Rain Cloud	Mary Rayner	Piccolo
The Patchwork Cat	Nicola Bayley & William Mayne	Picture Puffin

PICTUREBOOKS FOR OLDER CHILDREN

Burglar Bill	Janet & Allan Ahlberg	Picture Lion
Timothy Goes to School	Rosemary Wells	Picture Puffin
Long Neck & Thunder Foot	Helen Piers	Picture Puffin
Bread and Jam for Frances	Russell Hoban	Picture Puffin
A Birthday for Frances	Russell Hoban	Hipo
Alexander and the Terrible, Horrible, No Good, Very Bad Day	Judith Viorst	Bluegum

TITLE	AUTHOR	PUBLISHER

RHYMING BOOKS

The Rungawilla Ranger	Dan Vallaley	Angus & Robertson
Tiny Tim	ed. Helen Oxenbury	Picture Lion
The Young Puffin Book of Verse	ed. Barbara Ireson	Puffin
I Like This Poem	ed. Kaye Webb	Puffin
Amelia Bedelia	Peggy Parish	Avon Camelot
Amelia Bedelia Helps Out	Peggy Parish	Avon Camelot
Knockout Knock Knocks	Caroline Anne Levine	E P Dutton
Eight Ate: A Feast of Homonym Riddles	Marvin Terbun	Clarion

EARLY CHAPTER BOOKS

Flat Stanley	Jeff Brown	Methuen
The Owl Who Was Afraid of the Dark	Jill Tomlinson	Magnet
Jeremiah in the Dark Woods	Janet & Allan Ahlberg	Viking Child Books/Puffin

TITLE	AUTHOR	PUBLISHER
SHORT STORIES		
A Necklace of Raindrops	Joan Aiken	Puffin
The Faber Book of Nursery Rhymes	ed. Barbara Ireson	Faber
Stories for the Under-Fives	ed. Stephen & Sara Corrin	Puffin
Stories for Five-Year-Olds and Other Young Readers	ed. Stephen & Sara Corrin	Puffin
Little Pete Stories	Leila Berg	Magnet
Oh, Abigail	Moira Miller	Magnet
Just Like Abigail	Moira Miller	Magnet
Ramona the Pest (and series)	Beverly Cleary	Puffin
The Julian Stories	Ann Cameron	Fontana
Clever Polly and the Stupid Wolf	Catherine Storr	Young Puffin
Polly and the Wolf Again	Catherine Storr	Young Puffin
Simon and the Witch	Margaret & Barry Stuart	Fontana
The Return of the Witch	Margaret & Barry Stuart	Fontana

Appendix II

Further reading for parents and carers

TITLE	AUTHOR	PUBLISHER
READING AND RHYMES		
From Talkers to Readers the Natural Way	Harold Hoskins	Ashton Scholastic
Reading Rescue	Gillert & Bernard	Australian Council for Educational Research (ACER)
Teach Your Baby To Read	Glenn Doman	Pan
Babies Need Books	Dorothy Butler	Penguin
Finger Rhymes		Ladybird
ABC/The Useful Book 2 Songs, Stories & Verse	Kindergarten of the Air	ABC
Dance & Sing	Graham & McKinley	Wigg & Son
Reading Through Play	Carol Baker	McDonald
ACTIVITY BOOKS		
Fun Learning for Littlies	Pamela Richardson	Martin Educational
You and Your Small Wonder	Merle B Karnes	American Guidance Services
Active Learning for Infants/Ones/Twos/Threes	Debbie Cryer & Harms Bourland	Addison/Wesley Publishing Company
Australian Guide to Good Toys	Don Lewis	Australian Hampden Fontana
Baby Play	Pat Petrie	Century Hutchinson
First Fun	S Gregory & D Melvin	Octopus/Conran

TITLE	AUTHOR	PUBLISHER

BEHAVIOUR MANAGEMENT

Babies	Dr Christopher Green	Simon & Schuster
Toddler Taming: the Guide to Your Child 1 to 4	Dr Christopher Green	Doubleday
The Secret of Happy Children	Steve Biddulph	Bay Books
How to Discipline Without Feeling Guilty	Melvin L Silberman & Susan A Wheelan	Research Press
The One Minute Mother	Spencer Johnson	Colombus Books
The One Minute Father	Spencer Johnson	Colombus Books
Discipline: An Approach For Teachers and Parents	Merrill Jackson	Longman Cheshire
Positive Parenting	Loraine Toms & Tom Levett	Nelson

SPECIAL SITUATIONS

The Hospitalised Child	Denis & Dene Klenzing	Prentice-Hall
Children and Parents in Hospital	ed. J Lend & S Harvey	Karger Basel
Raising Children Bilingually	Lenore Arnberg	Multilingual Matters

Appendix III

Bibliography

TITLE	AUTHOR	PUBLISHER
Talk with your Child	Harvey S Wiener	Penguin
Learning to Talk	Bochner, Price, Salamon	Macquarie University
It Takes Two to Talk	A Manolson	Hanen Resource Centre, Ontario
TV and Your Child	Carmen Luke	Angus & Robertson
Articulation Development in Children Aged Three to Nine Years	Kilminster & Laird	Australian Journal of Human Communications, 1983

Index

A

action rhymes 57
action words (verbs) 25, 32
active play 49
adjectives 36
articulation 15–16
asking for things 10, 31
attentive listening 57
attitudes 49

B

babbling 19–21
babies 13–14, 19–21
    books 61
    toys 52
baby talk 28
bath books 62
behaviour 87–98
bilingualism 78–83
blocks, building 51–4
board books 62
body language 18
books 61–71
    for baby 21
    list 112–21
    making 64
bottles 100–3
bubble blowing 51
building blocks 51–4

C

capital letters 66
changing nappies 30
chatter
    babies' 20
    toddlers' 27
choices, freedom to make 50
code switching (biling-
        ualism) 79
colours
    concept of 30

mistakes 35
play 49
toys 51
commands 91–2
communication skills 15–18
    importance 9
complexity 14, 51
comprehension 17–18
computers 109–10
concepts
    learning 30–1
    role of TV 74
consequences 92
consistency 92
consonants
    development 45
    learning 40–2
    omission 38
    reading 71
constructive play 49
coordination
    oral 109
    role of play 49
copying 27
correcting mistakes see errors
counting 30
criticism 28
crying 19, 21

D

dance 58
decision-making 11–12
difference, understanding
    errors 36
    learning 89
    toys 51
discipline 87, 93–8
disputes 93
distraction 96–7
'doing' 35
dribbling 104
dummies 100–3

E

ear, nose and throat
        problems 99–100
emotions, expressing 10
enquiring mind 10
enthusiasm 28
errors
    grammatical 32–6
    pronunciation 28–9, 38–9
expectations of behaviour 95
exploratory play 49
expression 18
eye contact 27

F

faces, baby's recognition of 19
facial expression 17
family names 68
feelings, expressing 10, 93
finger play
    hand-eye coordination 49
    music 57
    role of books 62
first words 22–5
five-year-olds 43
fluency, lack of 108
four-year-olds 32
friends, making 11
frustration 96

G

games 47–54
    baby 22
    correcting pronunciation 38–9
    sound 58
gazing 21
genders 35
gestures 17
grammar 17, 27, 32–6
grouping words 36

H

hand–eye coordination 49
hearing
    loss 109
    problems 100, 107
help, asking for 11
hospital 104–6

I

'I' 35
ignoring behaviour 96
imaginative play 11, 49–50
imitation
    play 49
    reading 66
information seeking 10
intellectual disability 108–9
intelligence 28
interest 28
intonation
    communication skills 18
    holding interest 28
    learning 23
    role of books 62
irregular forms (grammar) 34
'is' 35

K

knowledge, relation to
    language 28

L

labels 68
language delay 109
language development 17
    bilingual households 78–80
    ear, nose and throat
        problems 99–100
    sick children 104–6
    twins 86
    use of computers 109–10
language problems *see* speech
    problems
language rules 17, 27, 32–6

lazy speech 108
lips
    baby's focus 19
    control 104
lisp 106–7
listening
    baby's skills 19, 21
    music 55–6
    selective 100
    to child 14, 18
location words 25
love 93
lower case letters 66
Luke, Carmen 73

M

make-believe 11, 49–50
'me' 35
meaning 23
memory
    role of books 62
    role of play 49
Menyuk, Dr Paula 14
mistakes *see* errors
modelling
    grammar 27, 34
    twins 84
modifiers (grammar) 25
moods 93
mouth
    coordination 109
    deformity 109
    muscles 106
multiple birth children 84–6
music 55–60

N

names
    first words 22, 25
    reading 68
    recognising concept 14, 32
    recognition 17
naughtiness 93–8
'no' 88
noise 14

non-fluency 108
nose problems 99–100
nouns names
number (grammar) 32, 35
numbers
    concept 30
    toys 51
nursery rhymes
    books 62
    listening skills 57
    speech improvement 30

O

objects
    play 49
    words for 25
one-year-olds 25
opinions, expressing 10
overstimulation 14

P

people's names 25
phonics 66, 71
photograph albums 62
phrases, learning to read 70
pictures 64
pitch 58
play see games
'please' 92
plurals 32, 35
pointing 21
politeness 11, 92
possession (grammar) 27, 35
post box game 68–70
praise 88
prepositions 36
preventing undesirable
    behaviour 97
pronouns 35
pronunciation
    baby 23
    correcting 28–9
punishment 97–8
puzzles 51

Q

questions
asking the child 27
by children 17, 32

R

rag books 61
reading 61–71
and talking 12, 64–6
and TV 76
learning 66
to baby 21
reasons, giving 97
relevance 22
repetition
first words 22
reading 66
requests to child 89
response 14, 27
rhymes *see* nursery rhymes
rhythm 55–60
importance 30
role of books 62
role-playing 11, 49
rules, games 51
rules, grammatical 17, 27, 32–6

S

scrapbooks 63, 70
self-esteem 93
sentences
baby 22
language development 17
learning to read 70
toddlers 26
sequencing (word order) 18,
27, 36
shape concepts 51
sick children 99–100, 104–6
sinusitis 99
size concepts

errors 36
play 49
slow talkers 31
social skills
development 11
role of play 49
twins 86
songs 58
sounds
awareness 57
baby's response to 19
learning to read 71
play 58
problems 108
speech 38–42, 45
space concepts, role of TV in 74
speech pathologists 38, 82,
104–11
speech problems (*see* also errors)
bilingualism 82
ear, nose and throat
problems 99–100
intellectually disabled 108–9
mouth muscles 106
reasons for 109
recognising 111
sounds 108
stutter 107–8
stimulation 14, 43
story-telling 17
structured conversation 14
stutter 107–8

T

tape recorders 58
television 72–7
viewing guidelines 75
tense 32
texture 49
'thank you' 92
thinking aloud 10
thinking independently 11–12
threats 92

three-year-olds
grammar 32
reading 64
speech sounds 38
throat problems 99–100
thumb sucking 100–3
tickling games 62
time concepts, role of TV in 74
time out 97
timing 30
toddlers 26–31
behaviour 88–9
music 58
play 49
toys 53–4
tone of voice *see* intonation
tongue
control 104
thrust 103–4
tie 106
tonsillitis 99
toys 51–4
twins 84–6
two-word sentences 26

U

upper respiratory infection 100

V

values 49
verbs 25, 32
video recorders 74
violence on TV 76
vocabulary, role of TV in 73
volume 58

W

warnings 92
weight concepts 49
word order (sequencing)
18, 27, 36